AF504398

Welcome

In the quiet of December,
as snowflakes start to fall,
Children gather 'round the fire,
hearing stories one and all.
Advent's season gently whispers,
with a promise pure and bright,
In each heart a hope awakens,
as we light the candle's light.

Little hands and eager faces,
eyes wide with festive cheer,
Listening to the tale of Jesus,
knowing Christmas time is near.
First a flicker, then a glow,
as the Advent wreath is lit,
In the warmth of this small flame,
in our hearts His love will sit.

Advent Adventures

Dedication

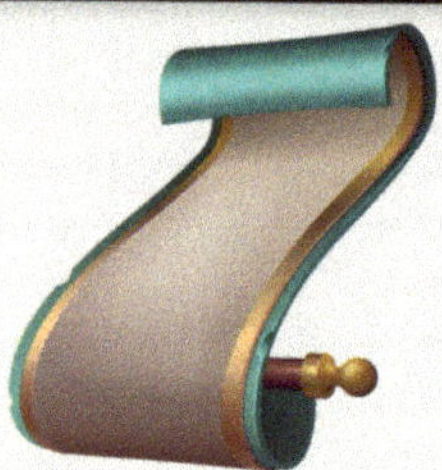

This Devotional Is Dedicated To:

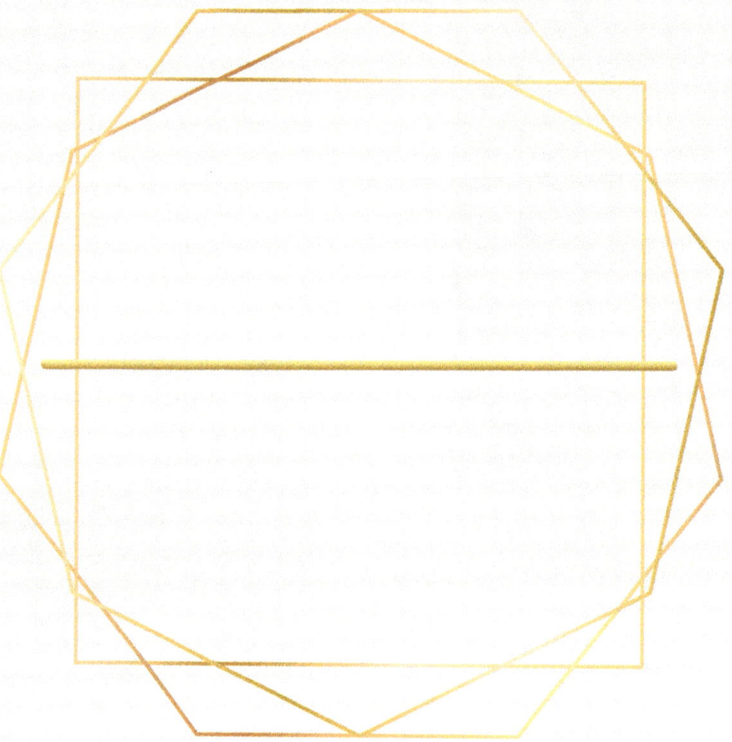

May these Advent Adventures bring joy, love, and a deeper understanding of the true meaning of Christmas to your hearts.

Family Welcome

Dear Family:

   This devotional is designed to help you and your child explore the true meaning of Advent. Each day will offer a meaningful and enriching scriptural experience for children.

Through engaging stories, thoughtful reflections, and creative activities, young hearts and minds will delve deeper into the true spirit of Advent, discovering the profound love and promise of God's gift to us."

Over the next 25 days, they will be embarking on a special journey, day by day, that brings them closer to the celebration of Jesus' birth. Each day, you'll find:

- *A Story or Lesson:* A new story or lesson that will teach about the love and kindness of Jesus.
- *Scripture Passages:* Verses from the Bible that show the way to live and love like Jesus.
- *Reflection Questions:* Fun and thoughtful questions to help them think about what they have learned and how they can use it in their lives.
- *Art Activities:* Creative simple projects that let you express your love for Jesus through art. Art activities are geared toward youngsters 5-9. Additional activities are included in the Art Activity 9-12 age level if desired.
- *Advent Songs:* Advent and holiday Christmas hymns dedicated to each day of the devotion.
- *Advent Facts:* Fun and informative historical information about the celebration of Advent.
- *Beautiful Illustrations:* Inspiring art that will help guide you on your spiritual journey, making each story come alive and helping you feel closer to Jesus.

You may choose to complete one devotional every day or choose a specific theme that would enrich your child.

May this journey through Advent bring joy and reflection to your family's holiday season.

Blessings,
Clare Rhyan-Wright

Family Together

Advent Adventure Begins

Dear Advent Adventurers,

Welcome to Advent Adventures: 25 Days Of Christmas Devotionals

We're so excited to have you join us on this amazing journey as we prepare our hearts for the most wonderful celebration of all – the birth of Jesus!

Over the next 25 days, you'll be embarking on a special journey, day by day, that brings you closer to Jesus' birth. Every day, you'll find yourself getting closer to Jesus. You'll learn more about His life and His love for us. You'll discover how acts of kindness and love can bring you nearer to Him and to each other.

To start our adventure, here's a little poem:

An Advent Adventure, day by day
With Jesus as our guide, we'll find our way.
Through stories, art, and joyful song,
We'll grow in love, and faith so strong.

Let's get ready for a wonderful adventure filled with joy, love, and the true meaning of Christmas. Together, we'll make this Advent season one to remember!

Are you ready? Let's begin our joyful journey to Christmas together!

With love, prayers and excitement,
Miss Clare Rhyan-Wright

The First Promise Of Hope

The Promise Of A Savior

Genesis 3:15 (Adapted)
"I will make you and the woman enemies to each other. Her children and your children will always fight. Her child will crush your head, and you will strike his heel."

Thought Of The Day

In the beginning, when Adam and Eve were in the Garden of Eden, they made a big mistake by not trusting God. Because of this, sin entered the world. God spoke to the serpent (the Evil One), who had tempted Eve, and told him there would be a constant struggle between good and evil. This struggle is like a battle.

God said that one day, a descendant of the woman would crush the serpent's head, even though the serpent would strike his heel. This means that even though evil might hurt us sometimes, good will always win in the end. Adam and Eve made a mistake but God still loved them very much.

He promised to send a Savior one day to save everyone from their sins. This Savior is Jesus, who came to show us God's love and to help us trust Him. It is important to trust God and listen to Him. Even when we make mistakes, God loves us and promises to help us. Always remember that God knows what is best for us.

Think And Pray

Why Do You Think God Promised A Savior?
Ask God To Help You Trust Him Even When You Think You Know Best.

Art "Adventure"
Promise Star

Cut out a star from paper and decorate it with glitter and markers.
Write "God's Promise" in the center and hang it in your room to remember His promise.

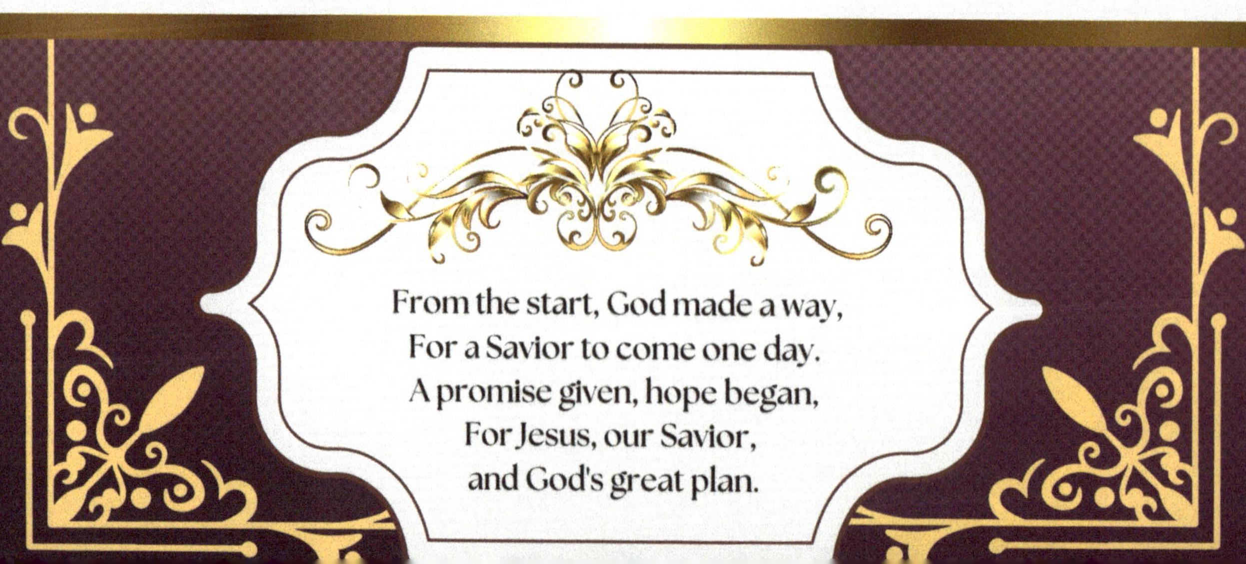

From the start, God made a way,
For a Savior to come one day.
A promise given, hope began,
For Jesus, our Savior,
and God's great plan.

Abraham's Promise Of Love

All Nations Blessed

Good News Reading: Genesis 22:18 (Adapted)
"And through your offspring all nations on earth will be blessed,
because you have obeyed Me."

Thought Of The Day

God promised Abraham that through his family, all nations would be blessed. This promise pointed to Jesus, who would bless the whole world. God keeps His promises and blesses those who trust and obey Him. Just as Abraham was blessed for his obedience, we too can share in God's blessings when we follow His ways and trust in His promises.

When we obey God , he uses us to being blessings for others. Just like Abraham' fath and obedience led to blessings for all people, our actions can have a positive impact on the world around us.

Think And Pray

How Do You Feel When You Receive A Special Promise?
What Special Promise Can You Make To God Today?
Ask God For His Blessings On The World Today

Art "Adventure"
Blessing Tree

Markers, construction paper, glue, scissors, yarn.
Draw a tree and add leaves with promises or blessings written on them.
Decorate the tree and hang it as a doorknob decoration to remind you of God's promises.

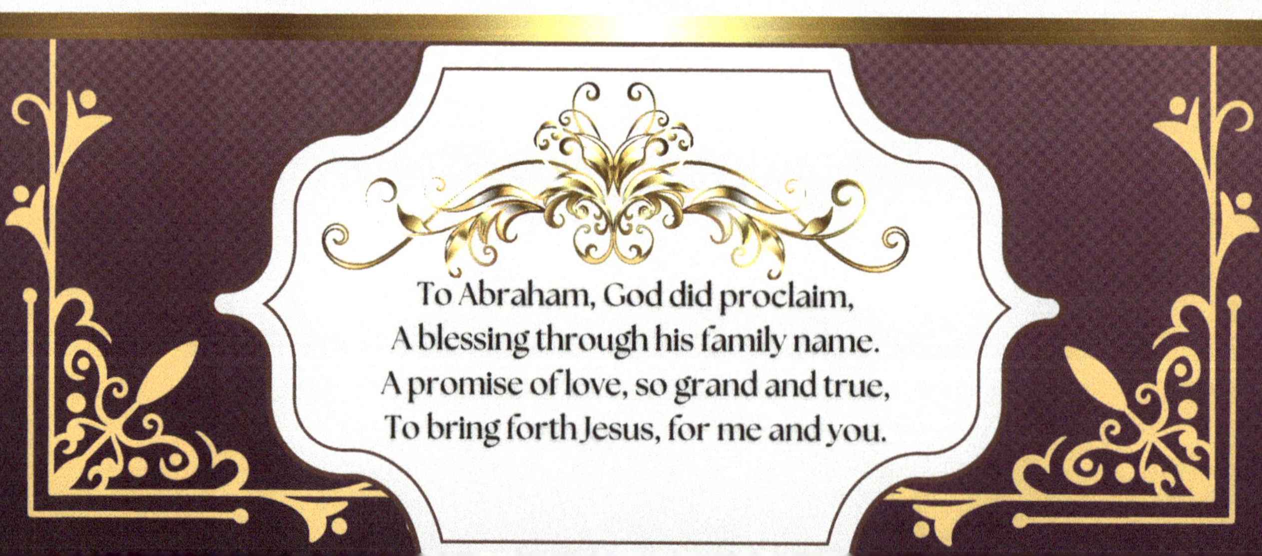

To Abraham, God did proclaim,
A blessing through his family name.
A promise of love, so grand and true,
To bring forth Jesus, for me and you.

Jacob's Star

A Star Shinning Bright

*"I see him, but not now; I behold him, but not near.
A star will come out of Jacob; a scepter will rise out of Israel."*

Thought Of The Day

Balaam was a man who lived long ago in a land called Moab. He had a special gift to talk to God (Prophet) and know what might happen in the future. A king named Balak asked Balaam to say hurtful things about the Israelites, who were God's chosen people.

But every time Balaam tried to say something unkind, only good words came out! God made sure that Balaam could only bless the Israelites, not curse them. This showed that God was protecting his people.

In the end, Balaam realized he couldn't go against what God wanted. He told King Balak that the Israelites were blessed and would be successful. Balaam learned that it's important to listen to God's plans, even when we might want to do something else. This story teaches us that God's plans are always best, and he protects those who follow him.

Think And Pray

What Do You Think The Star Of Jacob Means?
Ask God To Help You Follow What His Plan Is For Today.

Art "Adventure"

Jacob's Star

Poster paper, scissors, markers, foil, stickers.
Draw and cut out a star.
Cover it with foil, and decorate it with stickers.
Hang it on your Christmas tree to remember the prophecy.

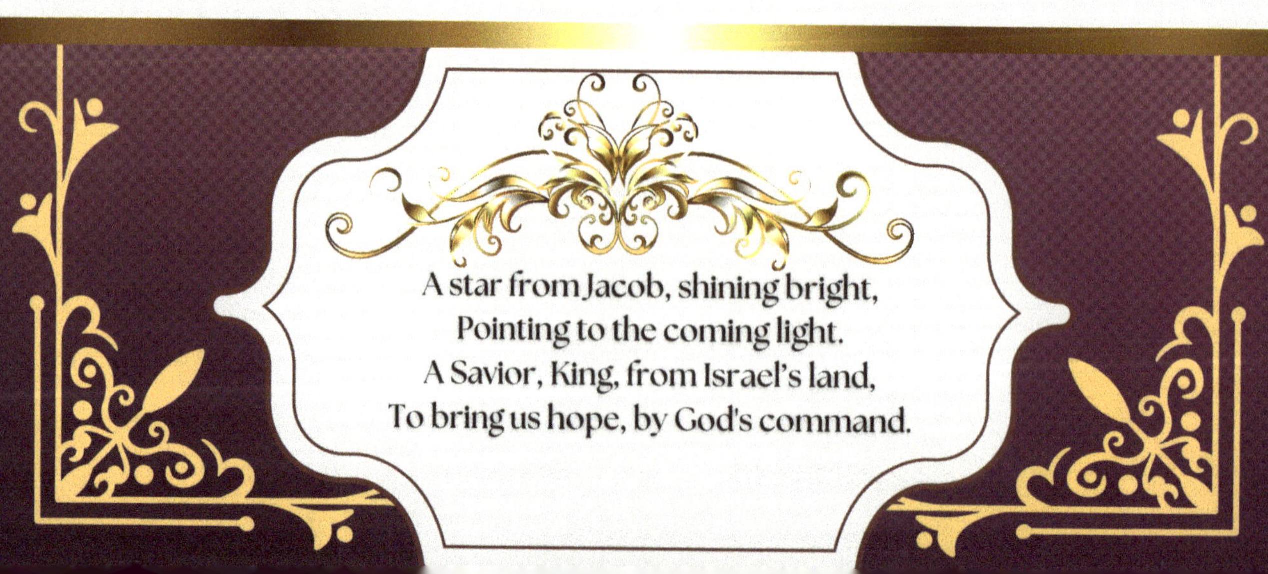

A star from Jacob, shining bright,
Pointing to the coming light.
A Savior, King, from Israel's land,
To bring us hope, by God's command.

David's Family Lives Forever

David's Throne Everlasting

Scripture Reading: 2 Samuel 7:12-13 (Adapted)

"When your days are over and you rest with your ancestors, I will raise up your offspring to succeed you, your own flesh and blood, and I will establish his kingdom.
He is the one who will build a house for my Name, and I will establish the throne of his kingdom forever."

Thought Of TheDay

God made a promise to King David that even after he was no longer alive, his family would still be special to God. God promised that David's son would become king and would build a beautiful place for people to worship God. And most importantly, God promised that David's family would always have someone as king, showing that God keeps his promises forever.

Jesus belongs to the family line of David. He is the King of Kings. God cares about families and keeps his promises. It shows us that God's love and plans for us can last forever, just like he promised to King David.

Think And Pray

Why Do You Think God Chose David's Family For Jesus To Come From?
Say A Blessing Prayer For Your Family.

Art "Adventure"
The Crown

Construction paper, markers, stickers, and glitter, glue.
Choose construction paper color.
Have help to measure your head.
Cut out crown shape and tape crown ends together.
Decorate your crown with glitter and stickers.
Wear it to remember that Jesus is the King from David's line.

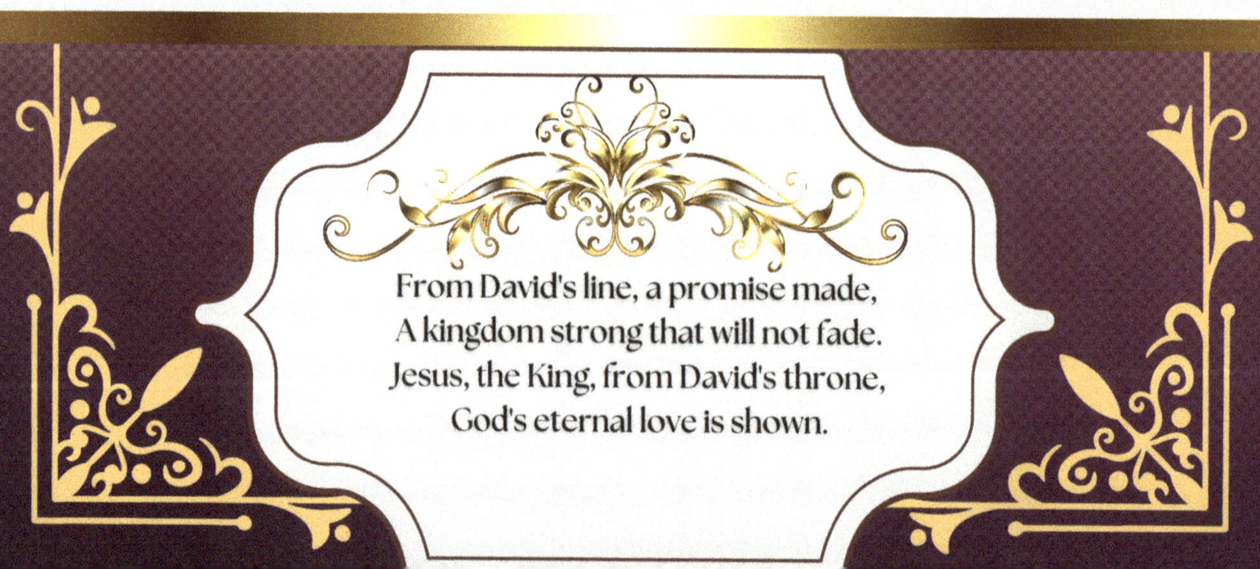

From David's line, a promise made,
A kingdom strong that will not fade.
Jesus, the King, from David's throne,
God's eternal love is shown.

Emmanuel

God Is With Us

Scripture Reading: Isaiah 7:14 (Adapted)

"Therefore the Lord himself will give you a sign: The virgin will conceive and give birth to a son, and will call him Emmanuel."

Thought Of The Day

The prophet Isaiah foretold that a virgin would give birth to a son named Immanuel, meaning "God with us." This prophecy pointed to Mary and Jesus. This name, Emmanuel, is really important because it tells us that God loves us so much that he wants to be with us all the time. So, when people heard this promise, they knew that God was planning something wonderful. He was sending someone who would help them know that God is always with them.

Later, this special baby was born, and His name was Jesus. Jesus came to show us how much God loves us and to help us understand that God is always close by, no matter what. This promise of Emmanuel gives us hope and reminds us that we are never alone because God is with us.

Think And Pray

What Does "Emmanuel" Mean To You?
Hold Hands And Pray Thanking Jesus For Always Being By Your Side.

Art "Adventure

Angel Messenger

Paper, markers, and glitter to make an angel.
Write "Emmanuel" on the angel.
Hang it where you can see it often.

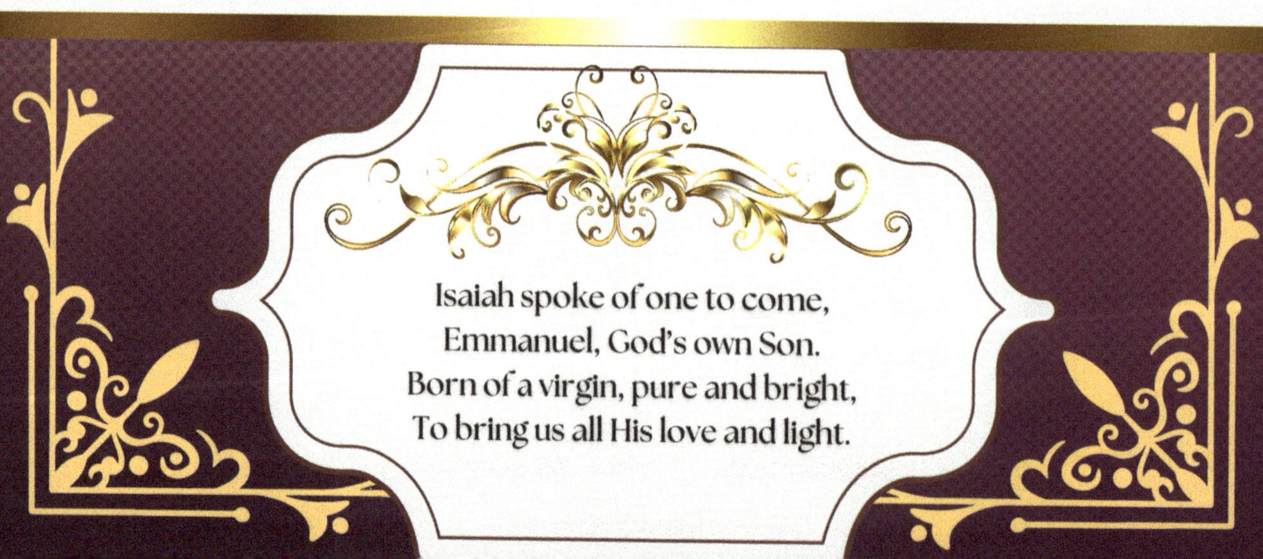

Jesse's Roots

Jesse's Branch Brings Life

'A shoot will come up from the stump of Jesse; from his roots a Branch will bear fruit.'

Thought Of TheDay

Isaiah also spoke of a Branch that would come from Jesse's family, bringing new life. This Branch is Jesus. This verse from the Bible is talking about a family tree, the family of Jesse. Jesse was the father of King David, a very important person in the Bible. Even though many years had passed and it seemed like the greatness of Jesse's family had ended.

God promised that a new leader, like a new shoot from a stump, would come from Jesse's family. This new leader is Jesus. Jesus, the shoot from Jesse's family, grew and brought good things to the world. We can do the same by growing in love and kindness, helping others, and sharing God's love with everyone we meet.

Think And Pray

What Do You Think It Means That Jesus Is The Branch From Jesse?
Pray To Ask God To Help You Grow In Love And Kindness.

Art "Adventure"

Jesse's Tree Branch

Use a real branch or draw one on construction paper.
Write favorite bible verses copied on construction paper leaves.
Attach leaves with bible verses that talk about Jesus.

____

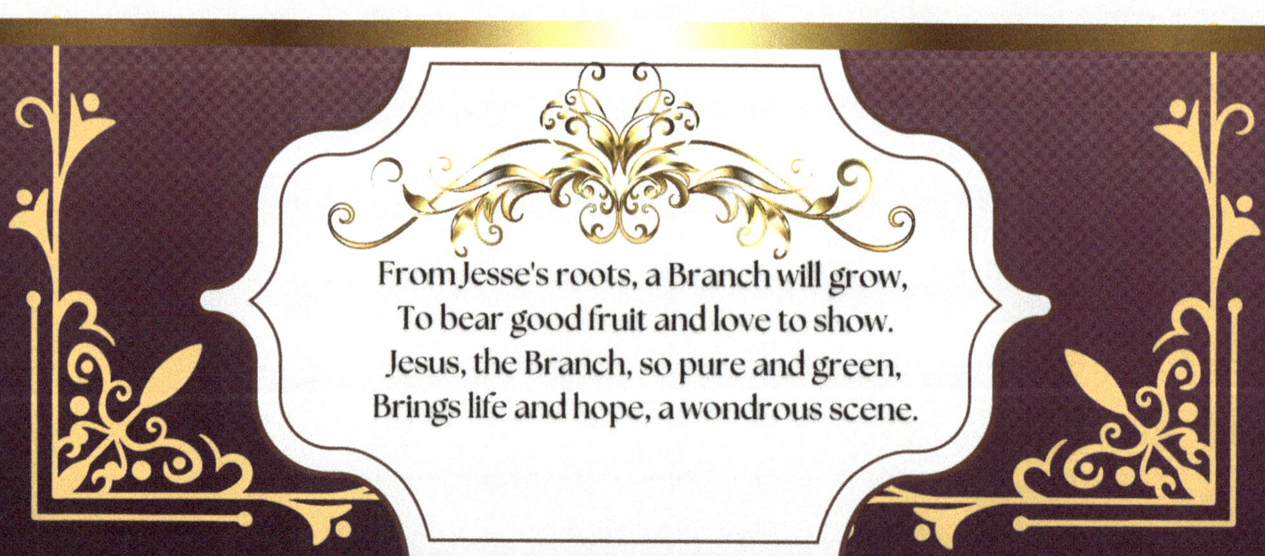

From Jesse's roots, a Branch will grow,
To bear good fruit and love to show.
Jesus, the Branch, so pure and green,
Brings life and hope, a wondrous scene.

A Small Town Bethlehem

Bethlehem Small & Meek

Scripture Reading: Micah 5:2 (Adapted)
"But you, Bethlehem, even though you are small, someone important will come from you.
This person will be a ruler over Israel, and has been part of God's plan for a long, long time."

Thought Of The Day

God used a small town like Bethlehem to do something very big and important. God sees and values everyone, no matter their size or importance. Just like God had a special plan for Bethlehem, He has a special plan for each of us. The verse tells us that from Bethlehem would come a ruler for Israel. This ruler is Jesus. Even though Bethlehem was small, Jesus, the most important person ever, was born there.

God keeps His promises in amazing ways. He has a plan for everyone, no matter how small or unimportant they might feel. Just like Bethlehem was chosen for something special, we each have a special role in God's plan.

Think And Pray

Even Though You Feel Small, What Can You Do To Bring Others Close To God?
Say A Prayer To Thank God For Sending Jesus To Be Our Ruler And Savior.

Art "Adventure"
Bethlehem 3D Scene

Paper, crayons, markers, glue, scissors.
Draw and color a picture of the town of Bethlehem.
Include houses, the night sky, and the star that guided the Wise Men to Jesus.
Cut out and glue the different parts onto a larger piece of paper to create a 3D effect.

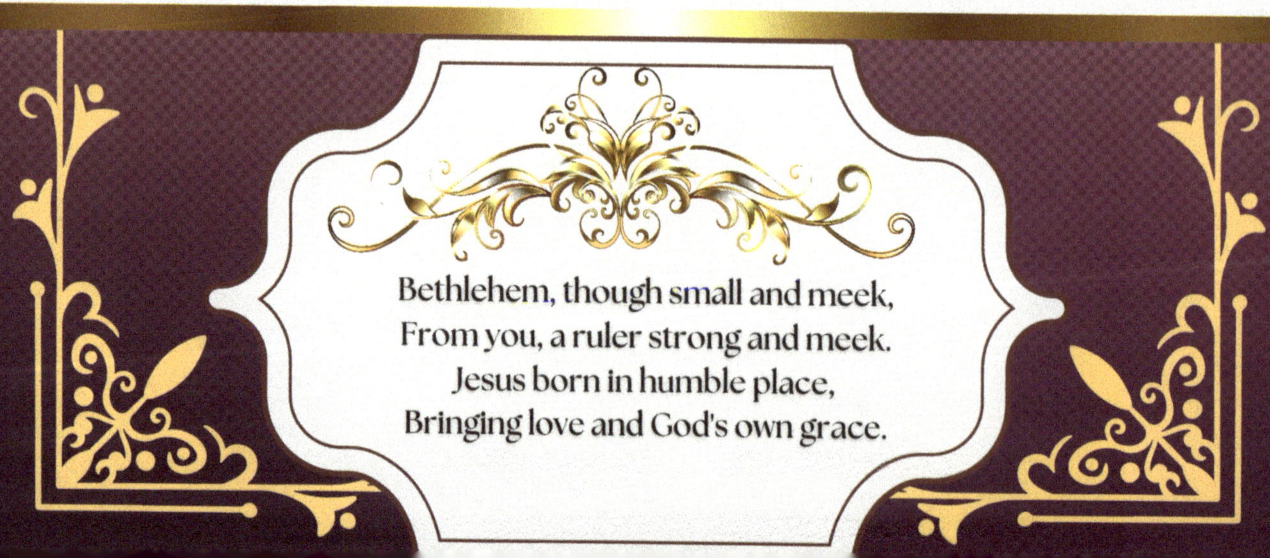

An Angel's Visit

Gabriel's Good News So Bright

Thought Of The Day

One day, the angel Gabriel visited a young woman named Mary. He had an important message for her. Gabriel told Mary that she was going to have a very special baby who would be the Son of God. Mary was surprised and a little scared, but she trusted God and was ready to do His will.

This news changed Mary's life forever. God Has a plan for you. Just like Mary, God has a special plan for each one of us. We might not always know what it is right away, but we can trust that He has something important for us to do. No matter where we are or what we are doing, God is with us. This means we are never alone and can always ask for His help and guidance.

Think And Pray

How Do You Think Mary Felt When She Saw The Angel?
How Would You Feel If God Sent You A Special Message?
Say A Prayer Of Thanks To Know You Are Never Alone To Ask God For His Help Always.

Art "Adventure"

Angel Ornament

Thick paper, cardboard, glitter, stickers, and markers.
Cut out an angel shape from cardboard or thick paper.
Decorate it with glitter, stickers, and markers.
Copy "The Lord is with you" on the angel's body
as a reminder of Gabriel's message to Mary.
Hang it on your Christmas tree to remember Gabriel's visit to Mary.

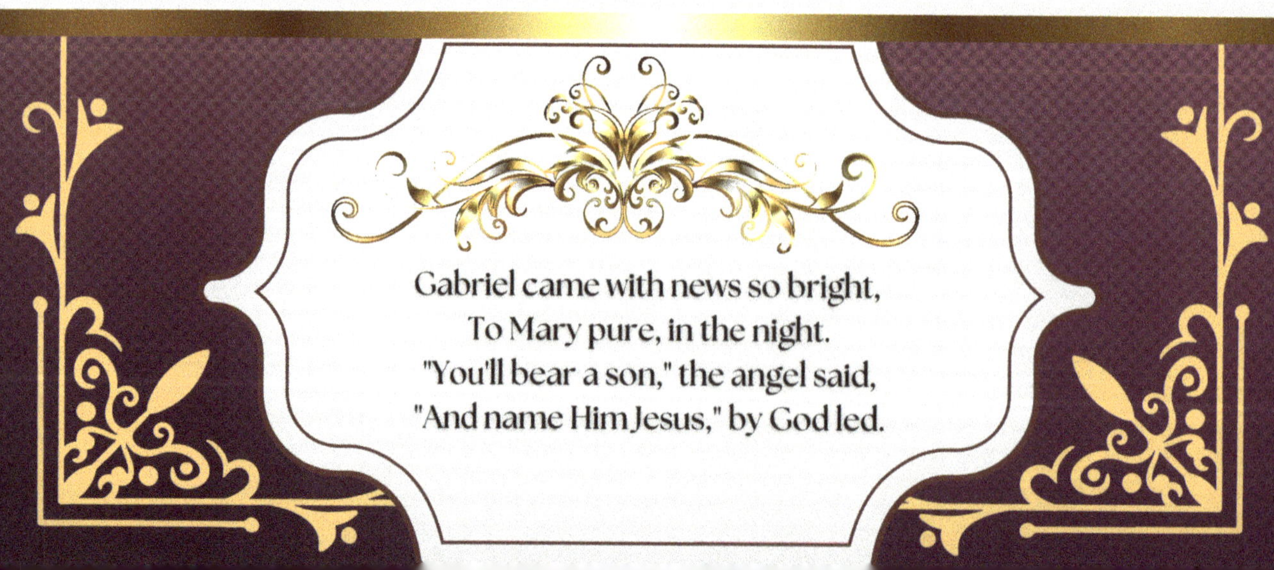

Gabriel came with news so bright,
To Mary pure, in the night.
"You'll bear a son," the angel said,
"And name Him Jesus," by God led.

Elizabeth's Baby Leaps For Joy

A Happy Greeting

Scripture Reading: Luke 1:39-41 (Adapted)

"At that time Mary got ready and hurried to a town in the hill country of Judea, where she entered Zechariah's home and greeted Elizabeth. When Elizabeth heard Mary's greeting, the baby leaped in her womb, and Elizabeth was filled with the Holy Spirit."

Thought Of The Day

Mary, who has just been visited by the angel Gabriel, quickly travels to visit her relative Elizabeth. Elizabeth is also expecting a baby, who will later be known as John the Baptist. When Mary greets Elizabeth, something amazing happens: the baby inside Elizabeth leaps for joy, and she is filled with the Holy Spirit. Elizabeth knew that Mary was blessed and that her baby would be very special.

Mary goes to see Elizabeth to share her news and to help her, showing the importance of family and supporting each other. Just like Mary and Elizabeth, it's important to support and care for our family members. When someone has good news or needs help, being there for them can make a big difference. Elizabeth being filled with the Holy Spirit reminds us that God is always with us, especially in important moments. We can feel God's presence in our lives when we are open to Him.

Think And Pray

How Do You Think Mary and Elizabeth Felt When They Saw Each Other?

How Do You Feel When You See Someone You Love?

Say A Special Prayer For Each Member Of Your Family.

Art "Adventure"

Family Greeting Card

Construction paper, crayons, markers.

Fold a piece of paper in half to make a card.

Draw a picture of Mary and Elizabeth on the front and write a message of love inside.

Give the card to a friend or family member to share the joy of Christmas.

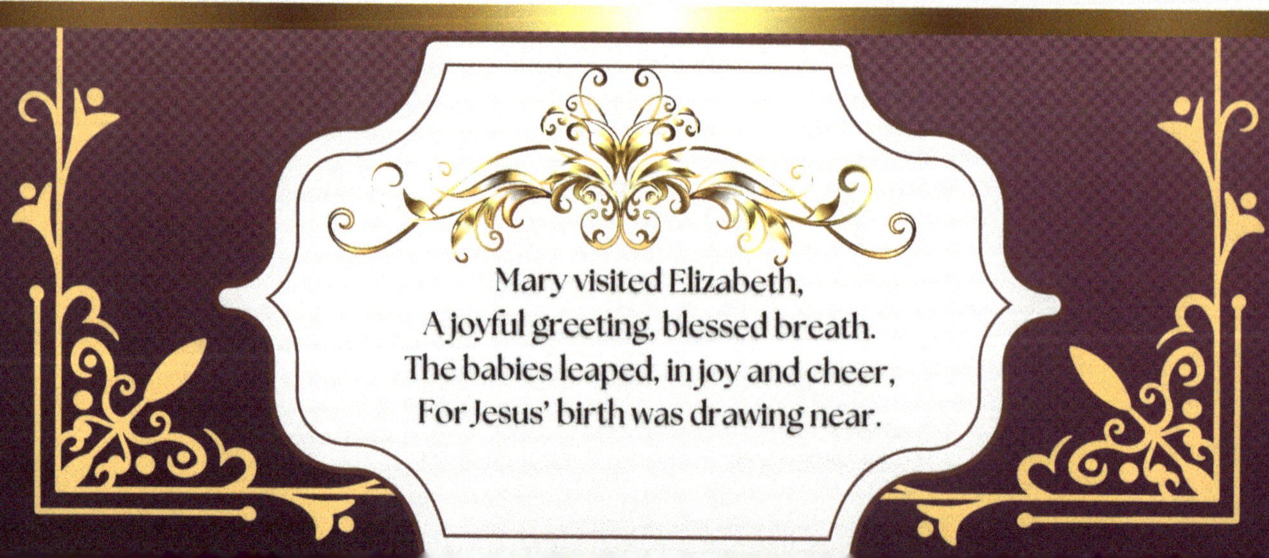

Mary visited Elizabeth,
A joyful greeting, blessed breath.
The babies leaped, in joy and cheer,
For Jesus' birth was drawing near.

John The Baptist
Prepares The Way

A Prophet Born To Lead

Thought Of The Day

Elizabeth gave birth to a baby boy, and everyone was happy for her. They wanted to name the baby after his father, Zechariah, but Elizabeth said he should be called John. This name was given by the angel and showed that John had a special purpose. This teaches us about listening to God and being brave enough to do what He asks, even if it's different from what others expect.

Elizabeth knew that God had a special plan for her son and that his name should be John. By following God's instructions, she showed faith and obedience. Sometimes, God asks us to do things that might seem different or strange to others. It's important to listen to God and trust that He knows what is best. Standing up for what God tells us, even when it goes against being popular, can be challenging. But like Elizabeth, we should have the courage to follow God's guidance and trust in His plans.

Think And Pray

Why Do You Think Elizabeth And Zechariah Were So Happy About Having A Baby?
How Did Elizabeth Show Her Trust In God?
Can You Think Of A Time When You Had To Do Something That Was Right,
Even If It Was Hard Or Different From What Others Expected?
Ask God To Help You Do The Right Choices Even If It Is A Hard One.

Art "Adventure"
Name Coat Of Arms

Water color pens, markers, thick colored stock paper.
Have help in finding out what your name means and
if there is a special story behind why you were given your name.
Draw a shield, write your name, and decorate a symbol to show the meaning.
Discuss how God knows each of us by name and has a special plan for each one of us.

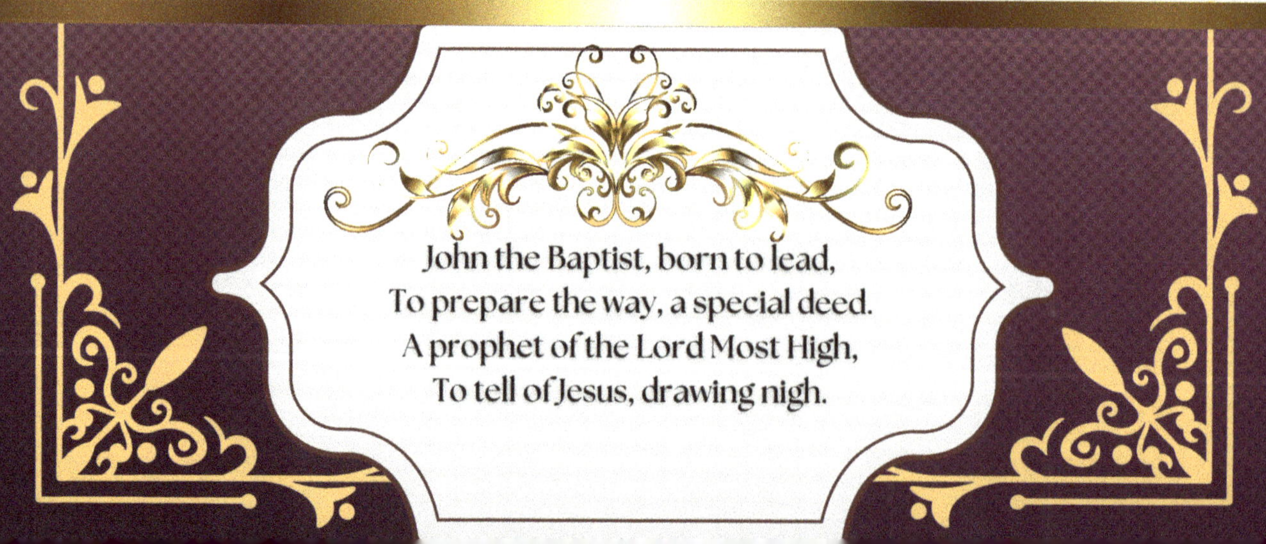

The Journey To Bethlehem

Travel To A Holy Place

Scripture Reading: Luke 2:1-4 (Adapted)

In those days Caesar Augustus issued a decree that a census should be taken of the entire Roman world. And everyone went to their own town to register. So Joseph also went up from the town of Nazareth in Galilee to Judea, to Bethlehem the town of David, because he belonged to the house and line of David."

Thought Of The Day

Joseph and Mary had to travel to Bethlehem because the ruler wanted everyone to be counted. It was a long and tiring journey, but they knew it was important. Little did they know, this journey was part of God's special plan. Joseph and Mary followed the decree and traveled to Bethlehem, even though it was a long and difficult way. This journey fulfilled God's plan, as it was prophesied that the Messiah (Jesus) would be born in Bethlehem, the city of David.

Sometimes, we have to do things we don't fully understand or that seem hard. By obeying, as Joseph and Mary did, we show that we trust in the bigger plan. Trusting that God has a plan for us helps us to be brave and do what we need to, even when it's hard. This story is about obedience and trusting in God's plan. Even when things are hard or inconvenient, following what is right and trusting that God has a purpose can lead to special events in our lives.

Think And Pray

How Do You Think Joseph and Mary Felt About Making This Journey?
Can You Think Of A Time When You Had To Do Something Difficult
But Knew It Was The Right Thing To Do?
Ask Someone In Your Family To Pray A Blessing Prayer For You.

Art Adventure
Journey Map

Bible Map, paper, markers, crayons, stickers.
Draw a map showing the journey from Nazareth to Bethlehem.
Mark the starting point and the destination.
Use markers and stickers to decorate your map.

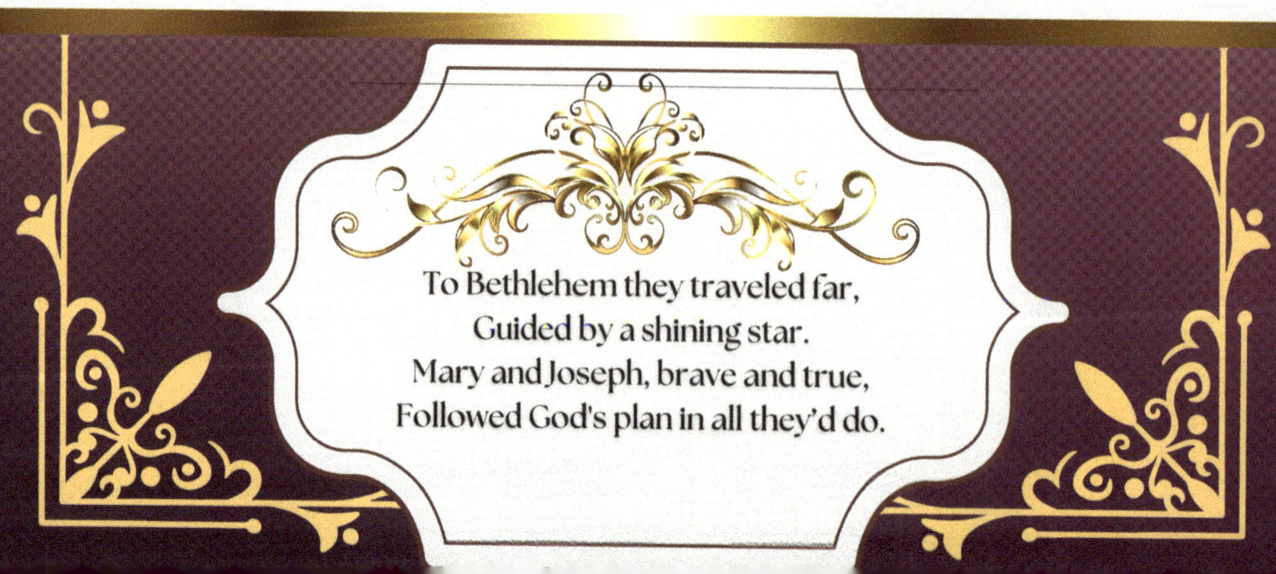

To Bethlehem they traveled far,
Guided by a shining star.
Mary and Joseph, brave and true,
Followed God's plan in all they'd do.

No Room At The Inn

No Place To Stay

Scripture Reading: Luke 2:6-7 (Adapted)

"While they were there, the time came for the baby to be born, and she gave birth to her firstborn, a son. She wrapped him in cloths and placed him in a manger because there was no guest room available for them."

Thought Of The Day

When Joseph and Mary arrived in Bethlehem, they couldn't find a place to stay because all the inns were full. They ended up in a stable where animals were kept. It was there that baby Jesus was born and laid in a manger. Mary gave birth to baby Jesus in this humble place. There was no fancy crib or warm bed. Mary wrapped Jesus in cloths and laid him in a manger, which is a feeding trough for animals.

Even though Jesus is the Son of God, He was born in a very simple and humble way. The story of Jesus' birth reminds us to be humble and appreciate the simple things in life. It teaches us to value people for their hearts and actions, not for possessions or status. We should always be kind and caring, no matter where we are or what we have.

Think And Pray

Why Do You Think Jesus Was Born In A Stable And Laid In A Manger?
What Can You Do Today To Be Kind And Caring?
Pray For Those Who Are In Need Of Our Love And Care.

Art Adventure
Manger Scene

Small box, hay or shredded paper, cloth, clay (for doll), or small doll.
Use a small box or a shoebox and fill it with hay or shredded paper.
Make a baby Jesus figure using clay, a small doll, or a rolled-up piece of cloth.
Place the baby in the manger.
Put the baby in a manger in your room as a reminder to be kind and humble.

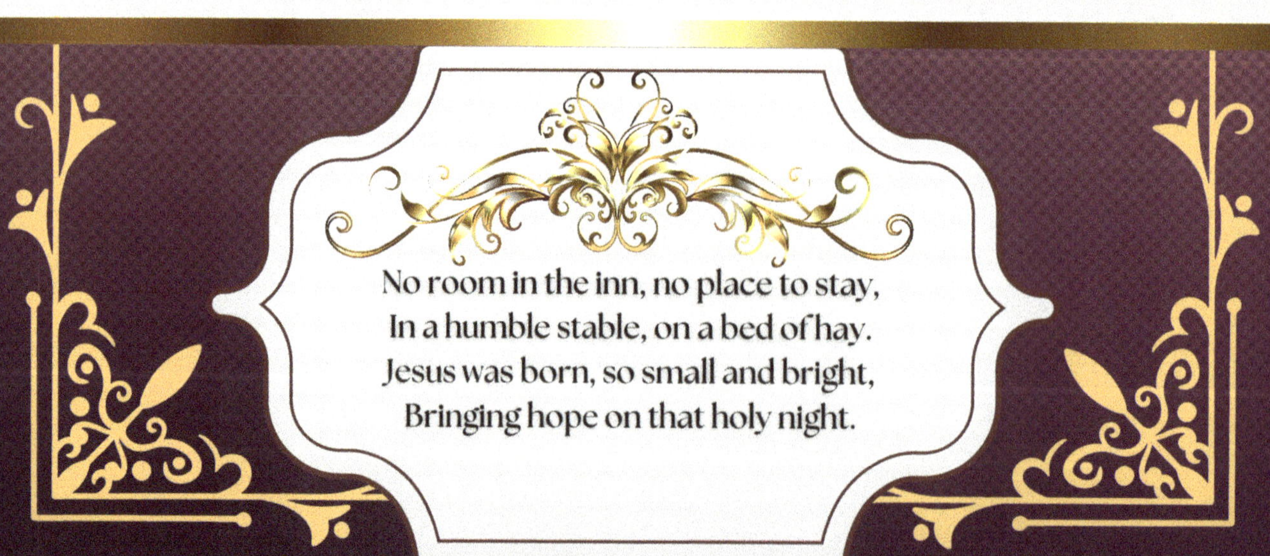

The Shephards & The Angel

Do Not Be Afraid

Scripture Reading: Luke 2:8-9 (Adapted)

"And there were shepherds living out in the fields nearby, keeping watch over their flocks at night. An angel of the Lord appeared to them, and the glory of the Lord shone around them, and they were terrified."

Thought Of The Day

On the night Jesus was born, shepherds were watching their sheep in the fields. Suddenly, an angel appeared to them with an amazing message. The shepherds were scared at first, but the angel told them not to be afraid.

Let's travel back to the fields near Bethlehem where some shepherds were watching over their sheep at night. These shepherds had an important job, making sure their sheep were safe from harm. The shepherds were ordinary people doing their regular jobs, but God chose them to receive the first news of Jesus' birth. This shows us that God values everyone, no matter how simple their life or job may seem.

The angel brought good news to the shepherds, and through them, to the world he story of the shepherds and the angel teaches us that everyone is important to God. It doesn't matter what our job is or how ordinary we feel. God has a special plan for each of us, and He can use anyone to share His love and good news.

Think And Pray

What Would You Do If You Saw An Angel?
How Can We Share God's Love And Good News With Others In Our Everyday Lives?
Pray Psalm 22 "The Lord Is My Shepherd".

Art "Adventure
Shepherd Puppets"

Craft sticks, fabric, glue.
Use craft sticks and draw shepherd faces on them.
Cut out small pieces of fabric to make clothes and glue them to the sticks.
Use your puppets to act out the story of the shepherds and the angel.

____

Shepherds watched their flocks at night,
Angels brought them such a sight.
"Don't be afraid," the angel said,
"Good news of joy is just ahead."

Good News From Heaven

Great Joy For All People

Scripture Reading: Luke 2:10-11 (Adapted)

But the angel said to them, 'Do not be afraid. I bring you good news that will cause great joy for all the people. Today in the town of David a Savior has been born to you; he is the Messiah, the Lord."

Thought Of The Day

The angel told the shepherds that a Savior had been born in Bethlehem. This was the best news ever! The shepherds were filled with joy and excitement. They couldn't wait to see baby Jesus.

The angel's message to the shepherds reminds us not to be afraid because Jesus brings us joy and hope. Even in times when we might feel scared or alone, we can remember that Jesus is with us and loves us very much. Just like the shepherds, we should share this good news with others and spread joy and kindness wherever we go.

Think And Pray

Why Do You Think The Shepherds Were So Happy To Hear About Jesus' Birth?
How Can You Share Joy And Kindness With Others Today,
Just Like The Shepherds Shared The Good News About Jesus?
Say A Prayer To Remember Jesus' Love And To Share His Joy And Kindness With Others.

Art "Adventure"

Angel Ornament

Thick paper, glitter, markers, and stickers.
Cut out an angel shape from cardboard or thick paper.
Decorate it with glitter, stickers, and markers.
Hang your angel ornament on your Christmas tree.

Good news the angel did proclaim,
A Savior born, Jesus His name.
Shepherds' hearts were filled with cheer,
For God's own Son was now so near.

Heavenly Choir Praises God

Glory To God

Scripture Reading Luke 2:13-14 (Adapted)

"Suddenly a great company of the heavenly host appeared with the angel, praising God and saying, 'Glory to God in the highest heaven, and on earth peace to those on whom his favor rests.'"

Thought Of The Day

After the angel shared the good news with the shepherds, a whole group of angels appeared, singing praises to God. The sky was filled with their beautiful songs. The shepherds were amazed and filled with wonder. The shepherds were in awe as they listened to the beautiful song. They felt a sense of peace and joy fill their hearts. The angels' song made them even more excited to see baby Jesus and share the good news with everyone .

The angels' hymn reminds us to praise God and be thankful for His love and peace. We can find peace in our hearts by trusting in God and remembering that He loves us very much. Just like the angels, we should share this peace and joy with others through our actions and words.

Think And Pray

What Song Would You Sing To Praise God For Sending Jesus?
How Can You Show God's Love And Peace To Someone Today?
Say A Prayer Thanking God For Sending Jesus To Bring Us Peace And Joy.

Art "Adventure"
Musical Shaker

Plastic bottle, rice or beads, a lid for the jar, stickers, markers.
Fill a small plastic bottle with rice or beads and secure the lid.
Decorate the bottle with stickers and markers.
Use your shaker to make joyful music like the angels did.

The Shephards Visit

Shepherd's Visit The Holy Child

Scripture Reading: Luke 2:15-16 (Adapted)

"When the angels had left them and gone into heaven, the shepherds said to one another, 'Let's go to Bethlehem and see this thing that has happened, which the Lord has told us about.' So they hurried off and found Mary and Joseph, and the baby, who was lying in the manger."

Thought Of TheDay

As soon as the angels went back to heaven, the shepherds looked at each other and said, "Let's go to Bethlehem right now and see what the Lord has told us about!" Without wasting a moment, they hurried to Bethlehem. The shepherds didn't hesitate or wait around when they heard the good news. They acted quickly and with excitement. They trusted what the angel had told them and hurried to see Jesus.

When you hear good news or feel that something is important, don't wait! Act on it with joy and enthusiasm. Just like the shepherds, be eager to discover and share wonderful things. It shows that you care and that you're excited to be part of something special.

Think And Pray

Why Do You Think It Was Important For The Shepherds To Go See Baby Jesus Right Away?
Can You Think Of A Time When You Were Excited To Share Something Good With Others?
Say A Prayer To Ask God To Help You Know To Act Quickly When Something Is Important.

Art "Adventure"
Shepherd's Staff

Ribbons, markers, construction paper.
Use a long stick or a rolled-up piece of paper.
Decorate it with ribbons and markers.
Use it to reenact the shepherds' journey to see baby Jesus.

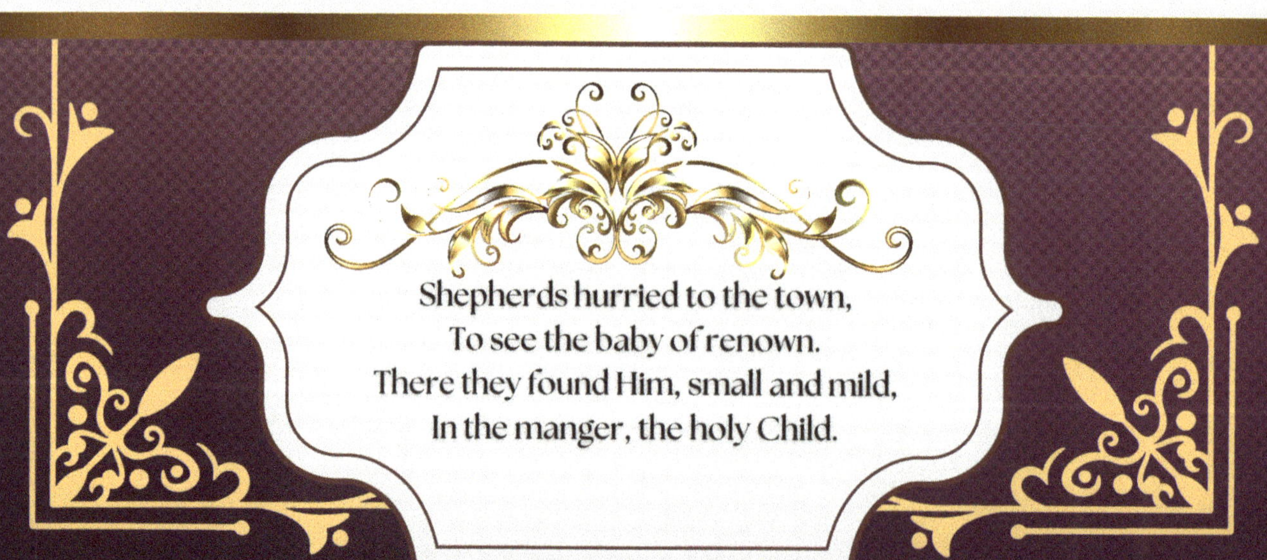

Wisemen Follow A Star

Star Gazers

Scripture Reading: Matthew 2:1-2 (Adapted)
"After Jesus was born in Bethlehem in Judea, during the time of King Herod,
Magi from the east came to Jerusalem and asked, 'Where is the one who has been born king of the Jews?
We saw his star when it rose and have come to worship him.'"

Thought Of TheDay

Far away in the East, wise men saw a bright new star in the sky. They knew it meant a special king had been born. They decided to follow the star to find and worship Him. The Wisemen were very brave and smart. They saw a special star and understood that it meant something wonderful had happened. They traveled a long way to find Jesus because they knew He was important and wanted to honor Him.

When you know something is right and important, don't be afraid to follow your heart and do what you need to do. Just like the Wisemen, be brave, curious, and determined. Seek out what is good and true, even if it's a long journey. Your efforts will be rewarded, and you will find joy and meaning in the end.

Think And Pray

How Do You Think The Wisemen Felt When They First Saw The Special Star?
Why Was It Important For The Wisemen To Follow The Star And Find Jesus?
Say A Prayer To Ask God To Help You To Be Brave And
Follow Your Heart To Do Something Important.

Art "Adventure"

Star Mobile

Cardboard, glitter sticks, markers, coat hanger, stick, string.
Cut out several star shapes from cardboard or thick paper.
Decorate them with glitter and markers.
Hang them from a coat hanger or a stick using string.
Watch them twirl and sparkle like the star the Wisemen followed.

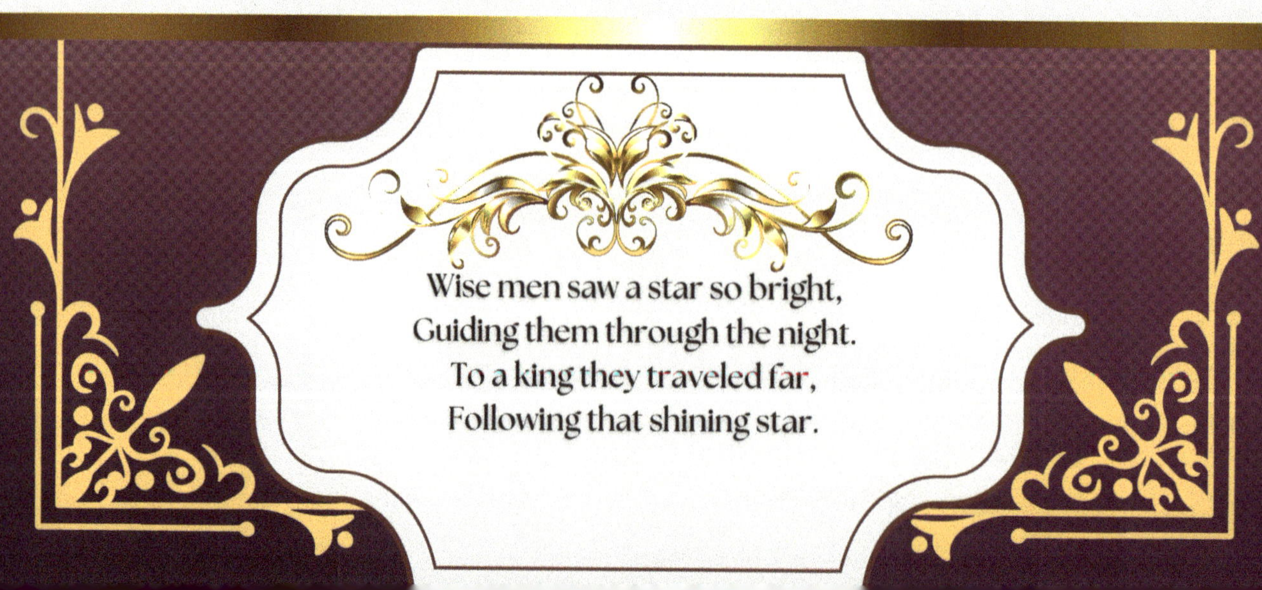

Wise men saw a star so bright,
Guiding them through the night.
To a king they traveled far,
Following that shining star.

A Royal Visit

Herod's Hall

Scripture Reading: Matthew 2:3-4 (Adapted)

*" When King Herod heard this he was disturbed, and all Jerusalem with him.
When he had called together all the people's chief priests and teachers of the law,
he asked them where the Messiah was to be born."*

Thought Of TheDay

King Herod was troubled because he was afraid of losing his power. Instead of being happy about the birth of Jesus, he felt threatened. He didn't understand that Jesus was a different kind of king who came to bring love and peace.

When we hear about something new or different, it's important not to be afraid or worried. Instead of reacting with fear, we should try to understand and learn more. Often, things that seem scary at first can turn out to be wonderful blessings. Like King Herod, we might feel worried, but we should remember to stay calm and open our hearts to new possibilities

Think And Pray

Why Do You Think King Herod Was Troubled By The News of Jesus' Birth?
How Do You Feel When You Hear About Something New Or Different?
Can You Think Of A Time When You Were Worried About Something,
But It Turned Out To Be A Good Thing?
Say A Prayer Asking God To Help You Be Calm When You Feel Worried
About Something New Happening To You.

Art "Adventure"

Crown

Thick paper, marker, glitter sticks, stickers.
Cut out a crown shape from cardboard or thick paper.
Decorate it with markers, glitter, and stickers.
Wear your crown and imagine being a wise person searching for Jesus.

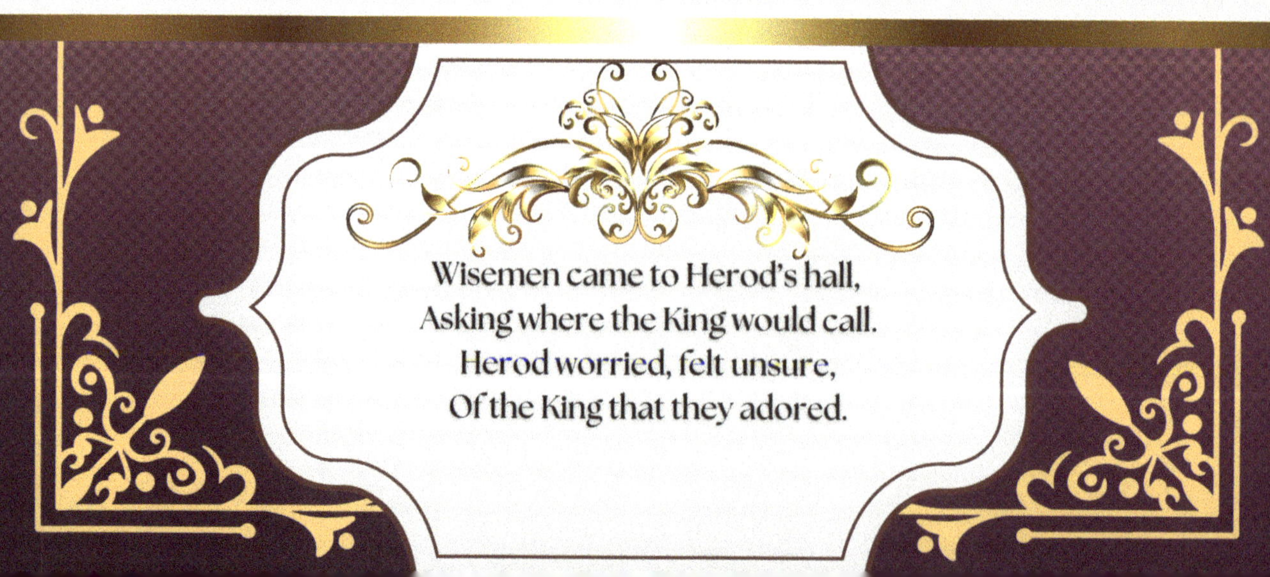

Gifts For The King

Bringing Treasures With Love

Thought Of The Day

The Wisemen traveled a long way, following the star with faith and hope. When they finally found Jesus, their hearts were filled with joy. They saw the child Jesus with his mother, Mary. They were so happy and amazed that they bowed down and worshiped Him. Then, they opened their treasures and gave Jesus wonderful gifts: gold, frankincense, and myrrh. These were very precious and special gifts, fit for a king.

When we find something or someone truly special, it fills our hearts with joy. We should be ready to give our best, just like the Wisemen did for Jesus. It's not always about giving expensive gifts; sometimes, the best gifts are love, kindness, and our time.

Think And Pray

How Do You Think The Wisemen Felt When They Finally Saw Jesus?
Why Did The Wisemen Give Jesus Such Special Gifts?
What Are Some Ways You Can Show Love And Kindness To Others?
Pray Today To Thank Jesus For Being The Special Gift In Your Life.

Art "Adventure"

Gift Box

Box, wrapping paper, stickers, and ribbon, and your gift.
What gift would you give to baby Jesus if you were one of the Wisemen?
Use a small box and decorate it with wrapping paper, stickers, and ribbons.
Place a drawing, a homemade gift, or a small toy inside as a present for baby Jesus.

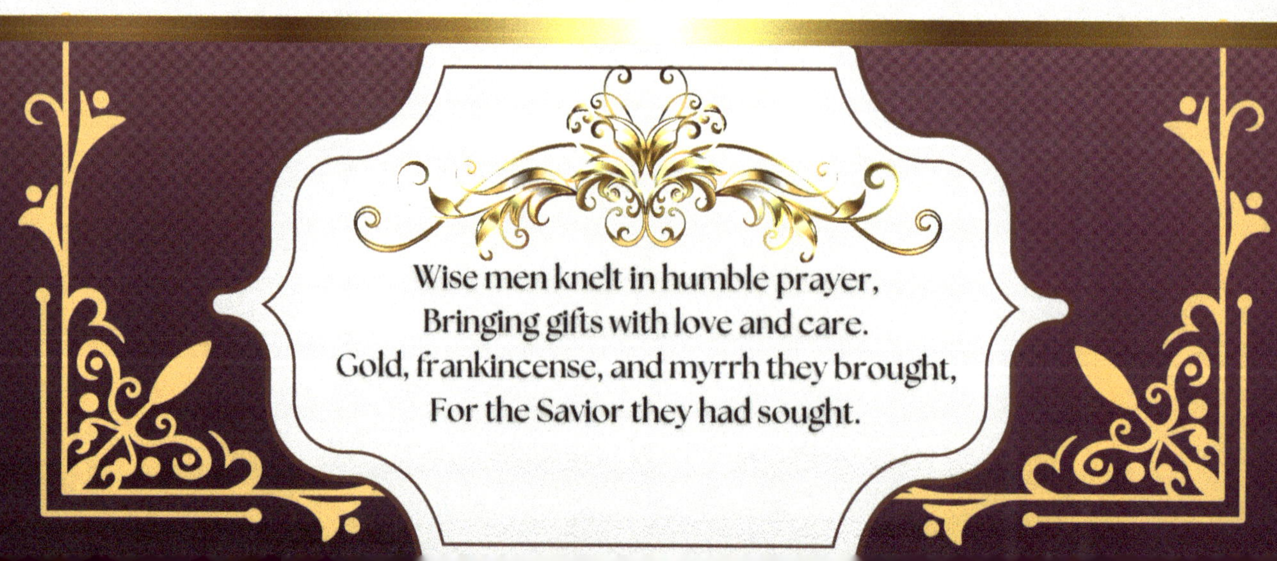

Journey To Egypt

Joseph Watchful Eyes

Scripture Matthew 2:13-15 (Adapted)

After the Wisemen had gone, an angel of the Lord appeared to Joseph in a dream. "Get up," the angel said, "take the baby and his mother and run away to Egypt. Stay there until I tell you, because King Herod is looking for the baby to kill him." So Joseph got up, took the baby and his mother during the night, and left for Egypt. They stayed there until King Herod died. This fulfilled what the Lord had said through the prophet: "Out of Egypt I called my son."

Thought Of TheDay

When King Herod sought to harm Jesus, God sent an angel to warn Joseph in a dream. Joseph obeyed immediately, taking Mary and Jesus to safety in Egypt. This shows the importance of listening to God and trusting Him, even when we must make difficult decisions or face uncertain times. Always trust in God's guidance and protection. Just as He protected the Holy Family, He watches over us and leads us to safety.

Think And Pray

How Do You Think Joseph Felt When He Had To Take Mary And Baby Jesus To Egypt?
Have You Ever Had To Trust Someone To Keep You Safe, Even When You Were Scared Or Unsure?
Say A Prayer To Ask God To Help You When You Are Afraid?"

Art "Adventure"

Holy Family Escape To Egypt

Travel Bag

Paper bag, markers, and stickers.
Decorate a small paper bag with markers and stickers.
Fill it with small items that you would take on a journey.
Pretend you are traveling to a safe place like Joseph, Mary, and Jesus.

In the night, they had to flee,
To Egypt land, by God's decree.
Joseph stayed, alert and wise,
Guarding them with watchful eyes.

Return To Nazareth

There's No Place Like Home

After Herod died, an angel of the Lord appeared in a dream to Joseph in Egypt and said,
'Get up, take the child and his mother and go to the land of Israel,
for those who were trying to take the child's life are dead. Having been warned in a dream,
he withdrew to the distric of Galilee, and livd a a town called Nazareth.
So was fulfilld what was said through the prophetd, that he would be called a Nazarene.

Thought Of TheDay

This story teaches us that God continues to guide and protect us. After King Herod died, God sent an angel to tell Joseph it was safe to return to Israel. Even though Joseph was afraid of the new king, God guided him to the town of Nazareth, where Jesus would be safe.

This shows that God cares for us and helps us find the right path, even when we are unsure or scared. Trust that God will always guide and protect you. He knows what is best for you and will lead you to where you need to be, just as He led the Holy Family safely to Nazareth

Think And Pray

How Do You Think Joseph Felt When The Angel Told Him It Was Safe To Return Home?
What Do You Think Jesus Felt When He And His Family Traveled Back To Nazareth?
Have You Ever Felt Scared Or Unsure About Something But Trusted Someone To Help You?
Say A Prayer Asking God To Keep You Safe And Bless Those Who Do Keep You Safe And Well.

Art "Adventure"

Holy Family Paper Plate Art

Air-dry clay or modeling clay in various colors, plastic utensils or clay sculpting tools, small piece of cardboard or paper plate for a base.
Make simple figures of Mary, Joseph, and Jesus using clay.
Roll small pieces of clay into balls for heads and larger pieces for bodies.
Use different colors of clay for their clothes and add details like hair, eyes, and other features.
Place the clay figures on the base, arranging them to look like they are traveling together.
Make a background of trees or a path using brown clay
for the ground and green clay for trees or bush.

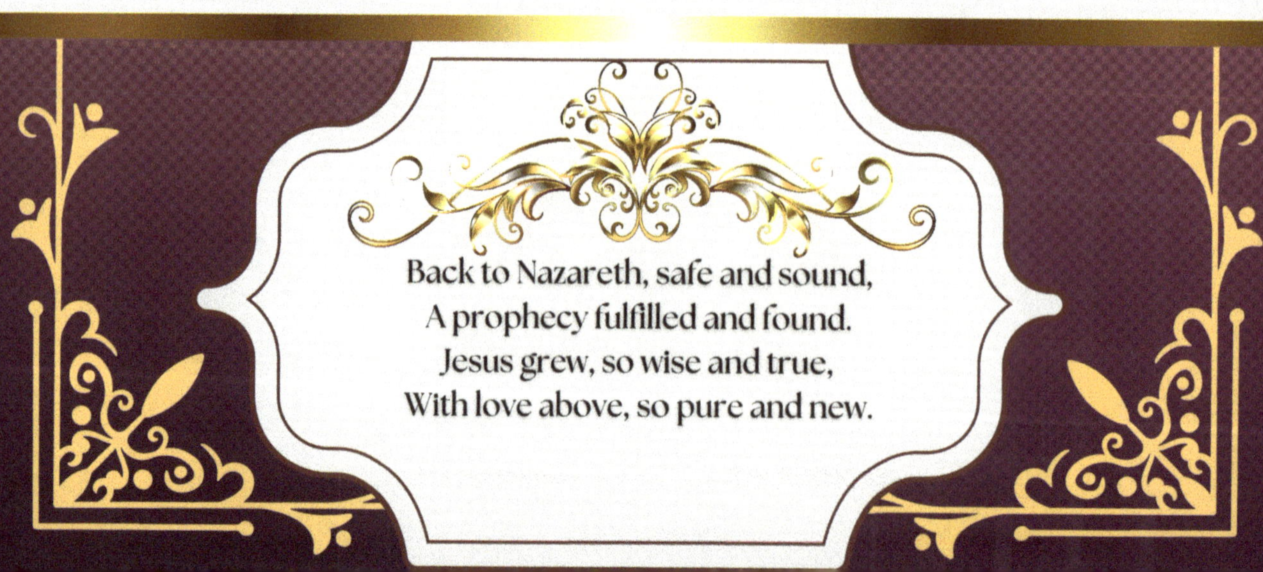

Back to Nazareth, safe and sound,
A prophecy fulfilled and found.
Jesus grew, so wise and true,
With love above, so pure and new.

Anna's Joy

Anna Waits No Longer

Scripture Reading: Luke 2:38 (Adapted)
"Coming up to them at that very moment, she gave thanks to God and spoke about the child to all who were looking forward to the redemption of Jerusalem."

Thought Of The Day

Anna was a very old woman who loved God and prayed a lot in the temple. When she saw baby Jesus, she knew He was the Savior. She was so happy that she thanked God and told everyone about Jesus.

Anna's story shows us how important it is to trust God and wait for His promises. She waited a long time but never stopped believing. When her prayers were answered, she was full of joy.

Think And Pray

How Do You Think Anna Felt When She Finally Saw Baby Jesus?
Why Is It Important To Thank God When We See His Promises Come True?
Say A Prayer Asking God To Help You To Be Like Anna,
Always Believing And Ready To Share Our Love With Others.

Art "Adventure"
Thank You Card

Construction paper (various colors), scissors, markers, crayons, or colored pencils, glue sticks, glitter (optional), stickers (optional).
Take different colored construction paper and cut out heart shapes.
These hearts will represent Anna's thankful heart.
You can make several hearts of different sizes.
Once all the hearts are decorated, glue the hearts together to form a chain or a garland.
Glue the tips of the hearts together to make a long line or
attach them in a circle to make a wreath.
Hang the thankful heart chain or wreath somewhere in your home or special place
as a reminder to always be thankful, just like Anna was when she saw baby Jesus.

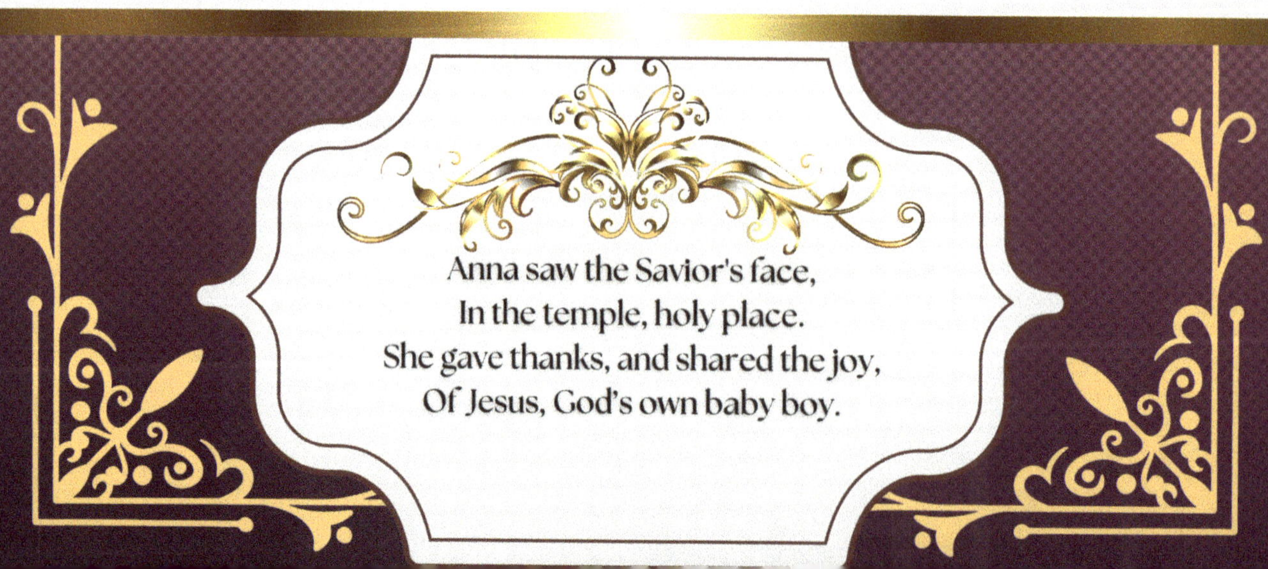

Jesus In The Temple

Heaven Watches With Loving Eyes

Scripture Reading: Luke 2:46-47 (Adapted)

"After three days they found him in the temple courts, sitting among the teachers, listening to them and asking them questions. Everyone who heard him was amazed at his understanding and his answers."

Thought Of TheDay

When Jesus was twelve, He stayed behind in the temple, talking with the teachers. After three days, his parents finally found him. Jesus was listening carefully and asking questions. The teachers were amazed at how much He understood and the answers He gave.

This story shows us that Jesus loved to learn about God and His teachings. Even as a child, Jesus was eager to share more about His Heavenly Father. It also shows us that asking questions and listening are important ways to learn. Be curious and eager to learn about God. Asking questions and listening carefully help us grow in understanding and wisdom.

Think And Pray

Why Do You Think Jesus Wanted To Be In The Temple, Learning About God?

What Can You Do To Learn More About God And His teachings?

Say A Prayer Asking God To Help You Be More Like Jesus,

Always Eager To Learn About Him And His Teachings

Art "Adventure"

Learning About God Book

Blank paper (several sheets), construction paper for the cover,
markers, crayons, or colored pencils, hole punch, ribbon or yarn.
Fold several sheets of blank paper in half to make a booklet.
Fold a piece of construction paper in half for the cover and place it around the blank paper.
Decorate the cover: Write "My Learning About God Book"
on the cover and decorate with drawings or stickers.
On the first page, draw or write about the story of young Jesus in the temple.
On the next pages, write or draw things you learned about God,
questions you have, or favorite Bible verses.
Punch two holes along the folded edge and tie with ribbon or yarn.
Fill in your book .

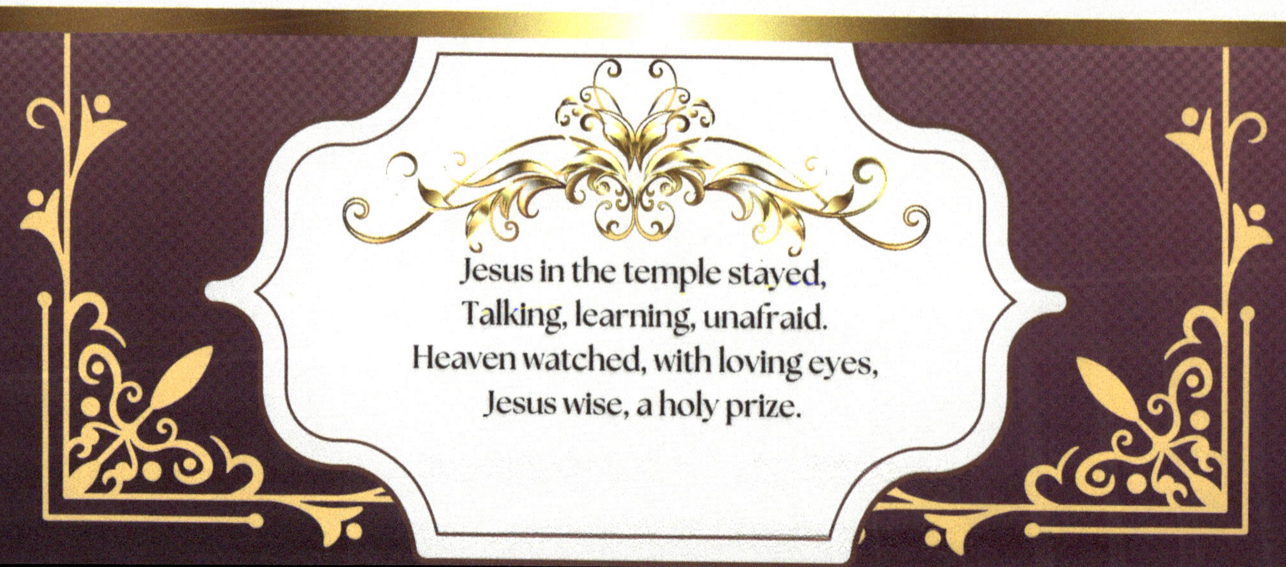

Jesus Grows Up

Learning, Growing, Day By Day

Scripture Reading: Luke 2:52 (Adapted)
"And Jesus grew in wisdom and stature, and in favor with God and man."

Thought Of The Day

As Jesus grew up, He became wiser, stronger, and well-liked by both God and people. Jesus didn't just grow physically. He also grew in His understanding of God and how to live a good life. This means that as we grow, we should also try to become wiser, healthier, and kinder, just like Jesus.

Think And Pray

How Can You Grow In Wisdom Like Jesus Did?
What Can You Do To Take Care Of Your Body As You Grow?
Ask God How To Be Kind And Make Good Friends.
Ask God To Help You To Grow In Wisdom Like Jesus Did.

Art "Adventure"

"Growing in Wisdom and Stature Chart"

Large sheet of paper or poster board, markers, crayons, or colored pencils, ruler, stickers (optional), pictures of things that represent wisdom, health, and kindness (from magazines or printed materials.
Draw three columns on the large sheet of paper or poster board.
Label them "Wisdom," "Stature," and "Favor."
In the "Wisdom" column, draw or paste pictures that represent learning and understanding (like books or a lightbulb).
In the "Stature" column, draw or paste pictures that represent growing strong and healthy (like fruits, vegetables, or someone exercising).
In the "Favor" column, draw or paste pictures that represent kindness and being liked by others (like friends, hearts, or helping hands).
Fill in the Chart:
Each day or week, write or draw something you did to grow in wisdom, take care of your body, or be kind to others. Add stickers or more pictures to each column .

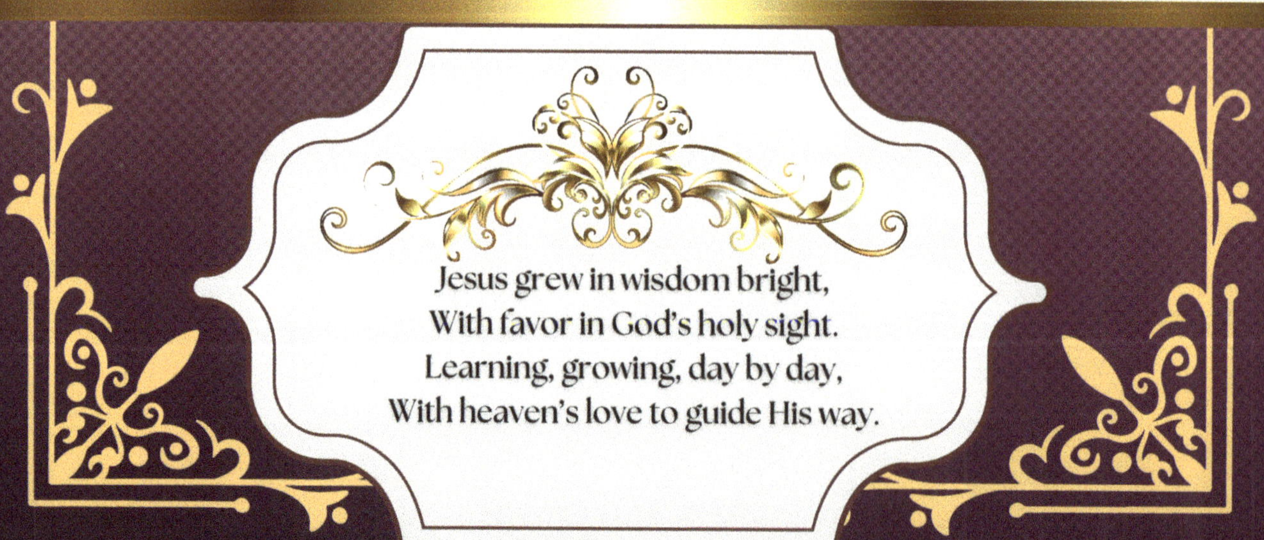

Jesus grew in wisdom bright,
With favor in God's holy sight.
Learning, growing, day by day,
With heaven's love to guide His way.

The Christmas Story
Is Our Story

Christmas Story Is Our Story

The Nativity Story Luke 2:1-20 (Adapted)

Thought Of The Day

Once upon a time, in a little town called Bethlehem, a very special baby was born. His name was Jesus. He wasn't born in a palace, but in a simple stable where animals were kept. His mother, Mary, and father, Joseph, wrapped Him in cloths and laid Him in a manger. This humble beginning was the start of a story that would change the world forever.

You see, the birth of Jesus isn't just a story from long ago. It's our story too. Jesus came to bring love, hope, and joy to everyone. Just like the shepherds, we are invited to share in this good news. When we celebrate Christmas, we remember that Jesus was born for us. He came to show us how much God loves us and to teach us how to love one another.

Every time we are kind, help a friend, or share what we have, we are living out the Christmas story. The love and joy that Jesus brought into the world are meant for all of us. That's why Christmas is such a special time. It reminds us that we are all part of this wonderful story of love and hope.

Think And Pray

Thank Jesus For Coming Into Your Life Today And Everyday.
Spend Time To Share A Gift, Special Word Or Act Of Loving Kindness As Your Gift To Jesus.

A Special Note Just For You

So, next time you see a nativity scene or hear a Christmas carol, remember that the story of Jesus' birth is also your story. It's a story of love that we can share every day, not just at Christmas. Because of Jesus, we know that we are loved, and we can share that love with everyone around us. That's what makes Christmas our story.

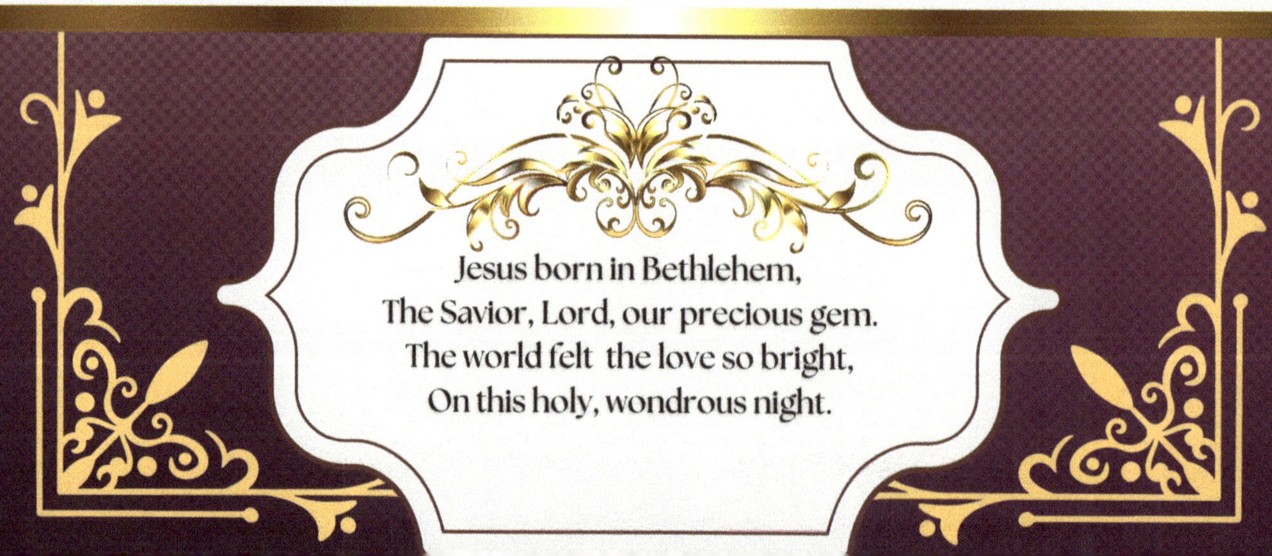

Art Projects Ages 9-12
Table of Contents

Art From The Heart

Art Projects Ages 9-12

Day 1:
Genesis 3:15 - Creation Of Promise

Materials Needed:
- Poster board or large paper
- Colored pencils, markers, or paints
- Scissors
- Glue
- Old magazines for collage

Instructions:
1. Read Genesis 3:15 together and discuss the promise God made.
2. Draw or paint a picture representing the promise. Depict symbols like a serpent, a woman, and the earth.
3. Create a collage using magazine cutouts to represent the struggle between good and evil and the promise of salvation.
4. Be creative and think about how God's promise gives hope.

Day: 2
Genesis 22:18 - Tree Of Blessing

Materials Needed:
- Construction paper
- Colored markers or crayons
- Scissors
- Glue

Instructions:
1. Read and discuss Genesis 22:18, focusing on the blessings given to Abraham.
2. Draw a large tree on construction paper.
3. On separate pieces of paper, write or draw different blessings in your lives.
   Cut out the blessings and glue them onto the tree branches, creating a Tree of Blessings.

Art From The Heart

Art Projects Ages 9-12

Day 3:
Numbers 24:17 Jacob's - Star
<u>Materials Needed:</u>

- Black construction paper
- Silver and gold glitter
- Glue
- Star-shaped templates or stencils

<u>Instructions:</u>

1. Read Numbers 24:17 and talk about the prophecy of the star.
2. Using star-shaped templates, trace and cut out several stars from black construction paper.
3. Apply glue to the stars and sprinkle silver and gold glitter over them to make them sparkle.
4. Arrange the stars on a large piece of black paper to create a night sky scene with the Star of Jacob is the central focus.

Day: 4
2 Samuel 7:12-13 King's Throne
<u>Materials Needed:</u>

- Cardboard or thick paper
- Paints and brushes
- Decorative items (beads, sequins, etc.)
- Glue
- Scissors

<u>Instructions:</u>

1. Read 2 Samuel 7:12-13 and discuss the promise of a kingdom.
2. Provide a piece of cardboard to draw and cut out a throne shape.
3. Paint and decorate their thrones using various decorative items.
4. Think about what it means for Jesus to be a king and how His kingdom is different from earthly kingdoms.

Art From The Heart

Day 5:

Isaiah 7:14 Emmanuel

Materials Needed:

• Clear plastic ornaments (available at craft stores)

• Small slips of paper

• Colored markers

• Ribbon or string

• Glitter

Instructions:

1. Read Isaiah 7:14 and discuss the meaning of "Emmanuel."

2. Write "Emmanuel" on small slips of paper, along with other names for Jesus.

3. Roll up the slips of paper and insert them into the clear ornaments.

4. Add glitter for decoration.

5. Tie a ribbon or string to the top of the ornament for hanging on a Christmas tree.

Day 6

Isaiah 11:1 Branch of Jesse

Materials Needed:

• Brown construction paper

• Green construction paper

• Scissors

• Glue

• Markers

Instructions:

1. Read Isaiah 11:1 and discuss the prophecy of a shoot from Jesse's line.

2. Cut out a large branch shape from brown construction paper.

3. Cut out leaves from green construction paper.

4. On each leaf, write names or titles of Jesus (e.g., Savior, King, Lord).

5. Glue the leaves onto the branch to create the Branch of Jesse.

Art From The Heart

Day 7
Micah 5:2 Town Of Bethlehem

<u>Materials Needed:</u>
- Blue construction paper
- White construction paper
- Scissors
- Glue
- Colored markers

<u>Instructions:</u>
1. Read Micah 5:2 and talk about the prophecy of Bethlehem.
2. Cut out a simple town silhouette from white construction paper.
3. Glue the town silhouette onto a piece of blue construction paper to represent the night sky.
4. Add stars and other details with markers to complete the scene

Day 8
Luke 1:26-28 The
Angel Announcement

<u>Materials Needed:</u>
- Paper plates
- Paints or markers
- Glitter
- Glue
- Scissors
- Ribbon

<u>Instructions:</u>
1. Read Luke 1:26-28 and discuss the angel's announcement to Mary.
2. Decorate a paper plate to look like an angel, adding wings, a halo, and glitter.
3. Cut out a small scroll shape from paper and write "Hail, favored one! The Lord is with you."
4. Attach the scroll to the angel's hands using glue.
5. Add a ribbon to the top of the paper plate for hanging.

Art From The Heart

Art Projects Ages 9-12

Day 9:
Luke 1:39-41 - Mary And Elizabeth
Materials Needed:
- Construction paper
- Scissors
- Glue
- Colored pencils or markers

Instructions:
1. Read Luke 1:39-41 and discuss the visitation of Mary and Elizabeth.
2. Draw and cut out simple figures of Mary and Elizabeth from construction paper.
3. Decorate the figures with colored pencils or markers.
4. Create a background scene on a larger piece of paper and glue the figures of Mary and Elizabeth onto it, depicting their joyful meeting.

Day 10:
Luke 1:57-60 - Baby Baptist
Materials Needed:
- Small paper bags
- Colored paper
- Markers
- Scissors
- Glue

Instructions:
1. Read Luke 1:57-60 and talk about the birth of John the Baptist.
2. Decorate a small paper bag to look like a baby, using colored paper to create a face and blanket.
3. Draw or cut out symbols related to John the Baptist (e.g., a cross, water, etc.) and glue them onto the bag.
4. Use the decorated bags as a reminder of the special birth of John and his role in preparing the way for Jesus.

Art From The Heart

Art Projects Ages 9-12

Day 11:
Luke 2:1-4 Journey Map

Materials Needed:
• Large sheet of paper or poster board
• Colored markers or crayons
• Stickers (optional)
• Scissors
• Glue

Instructions:
1. Read Luke 2:1-4 and discuss Mary and Joseph's journey to Bethlehem.
2 Draw a map of their journey, including important stops and landmarks.
3. Decorate the map with drawings, markers, and stickers to make it colorful and detailed.
4. Encourage them to think about the long journey and how Mary and Joseph trusted God along the way.

Day 12:
Luke2: 6-7 Manger Scene

Materials Needed:
• Shoebox or small cardboard box
• Construction paper
• Scissors
• Glue
• Straw or shredded paper
• Small figurines or clay to make figures

Instructions:
1. Read Luke 2:6-7 and discuss the humble birth of Jesus.
2. Use a shoebox or small cardboard box to create a manger scene.
3. Line the box with straw or shredded paper to represent the bedding.
4. Create small figurines of Mary, Joseph, and baby Jesus using construction paper or clay.
5. Arrange the figures in the manger scene to depict the birth of Jesus.

Art From The Heart

<u>Art Projects Ages 9-12</u>

Day 13:

Luke 2:8-9 - Shepherds And Sheep

Materials Needed:

- Cotton balls
- Construction paper
- Glue
- Scissors
- Markers

IInstructions:

1. Read Luke 2:8-9 and discuss the shepherds in the fields.
2. Cut out shapes of sheep from construction paper.
3. Glue cotton balls onto the sheep shapes to create a fluffy texture.
4. Draw and cut out shepherd figures and decorate them with markers.
5. Create a background scene with the shepherds and their sheep in a green pape field.

Day 14:

Luke 2:10-11- Angel Message

Materials Needed:

- Construction paper
- Scissors
- Glue
- Colored markers or crayons
- Gold and silver glitter

Instructions:

1. Read Luke 2:10-11 and discuss the angel's message to the shepherds.
2. Draw and cut out an angel figure from construction paper.
3. Decorate the angel with markers, crayons, and glitter to make it sparkle.
4. Write "Good news of great joy!" on a small piece of paper and glue it in the angel's hands as a banner.
5. Create a background scene of the night sky with stars and place the angel in it.

Art From The Heart

<u>Art Projects Ages 9-12</u>

Day 15
Luke 2:13-14 Heavenly Choir
Materials Needed:
• Construction paper
• Scissors
• Glue
• Markers
• Cotton balls
Instructions:
1. Read Luke 2:13-14 and discuss the heavenly choir of angels.
2. Draw and cut out multiple angel figures from construction paper.
3. Decorate the angels with markers and add cotton balls for the wings.
4. Arrange the angels on a large piece of construction paper to create a heavenly choir scene.
5. Add musical notes around the angels to symbolize their singing.

Day 16
 Luke 2:15-16 Shepherd's Water Color
Materials Needed:
• Watercolor paper
• Watercolor paints
• Brushes
• Pencils
Instructions:
1. Read Luke 2:15-16 and discuss the shepherds visiting the manger.
2. Lightly sketch a scene of the shepherds visiting baby Jesus.
3. Use watercolor paints to fill in the scene, blending colors to create a serene nighttime setting.
4. Let the paintings dry and then display them to remind everyone of the shepherds' joy upon seeing
    Jesus.

Art From The Heart

Art Projects Ages 9-12

Day 17

Matthew 2:1-2 Wisemen's Journey

Materials Needed:

- Construction paper
- Colored pencils or markers
- Glitter
- Glue
- Scissors

Instructions:

1. Read Matthew 2:1-2 and discuss the journey of the wise men.
2. Draw a map depicting the Wisemen's journey to Bethlehem.
3. Decorate the map with stars and glitter to highlight the path they followed.
4. Add small cutouts of the Wisemen and their camels along the journey.

Day 18

Matthew 2: 3-4 - King Herod's Palace

Materials Needed:

- Shoebox
- Construction paper
- Scissors
- Glue
- Paints and brushes

Instructions:

1. Read Matthew 2:3-4 and discuss King Herod's reaction to the news of Jesus' birth.
2. Use a shoebox to create a diorama of King Herod's palace.
3. Paint the interior of the shoebox to look like a palace setting.
4. Cut out and decorate figures of King Herod, wise men, and palace guards.
5. Arrange the figures inside the shoebox to depict the scene where King Herod learns of the new king.

Art From The Heart

Art Projects Ages 9-12

Day 19
Matthew 2:10-11 Gifts Of The Magi
Materials Needed:
• Small boxes (like jewelry boxes)
• Gold, frankincense, and myrrh replicas (can be made from clay or small trinkets)
• Paints
• Markers
Instructions:
1. Read Matthew 2:10-11 and discuss the gifts the Wise men brought to Jesus.
2. Provide small boxes to decorate as the gifts of the magi.
3. Paint the boxes and label them as gold, frankincense, and myrrh.
4. Place small replicas or representations of each gift inside the boxes.
5. Discuss the significance of each gift and its meaning.

Day 20
Matthew 2:13-15 Escape To Egypt
Materials Needed:
• Large paper or poster board
• Colored pencils or markers
• Scissors
• Glue
Instructions:
1. Read Matthew 2:13-15 and discuss the flight to Egypt.
2. Draw a large scene depicting Mary, Joseph, and baby Jesus traveling to Egypt.
3. Add elements like a donkey, desert landscape, and palm trees to the scene.
4. Cut out and glue the figures onto the background, creating a layered effect.
5. Discuss the journey and the protection God provided to the Holy Family.

Art From The Heart

Art Projects Ages 9-12

Day 21
Matthew 2: 19-23 Return To Nazareth

Materials Needed:
- Construction paper
- Scissors
- Glue
- Markers or crayons

Instructions:
1. Read Matthew 2:19-23 and talk about the return to Nazareth.
2. Draw and cut out figures of Mary, Joseph, and Jesus.
3. Create a background scene of Nazareth on a larger piece of paper.
4. Glue the figures onto the background, showing the family settling back into their home.
5. Discuss how Jesus grew up in Nazareth and what it might have been like for Him.

Day 22
Luke 2:38 Anna's Joy

Materials Needed:
- Construction paper
- Scissors
- Glue
- Colored markers or crayons

Instructions:
1. Read Luke 2:38 and discuss Anna's prophecy.
2. Draw and cut out a figure of Anna holding baby Jesus.
3. Create a temple background on a larger piece of paper and glue the figure of Anna onto it.
4. Write Anna's prophecy on a piece of paper and attach it to the scene.
5. Discuss the impotance of the prophecy and howAnna knew about Jesus as Savior.

Art From The Heart

Day 23
Luke 2:46-47 Jesus In The Temple

Materials Needed:
• Clay or playdough
• Construction paper
• Markers

Instructions:
1. Read Luke 2:46-47 and discuss Jesus teaching in the temple.
2. Create a clay or playdough model of the temple.
3. Draw and cut out small figures of Jesus and the teachers from construction paper.
4. Place the figures around the clay temple to recreate the scene.
5. Discuss the wisdom of Jesus even as a child and how He amazed the teachers with His understanding.

Day 24
Luke 2:52 Jesus Grows

Materials Needed:
• Poster board
• Photos or drawings of a child growing up
• Markers or crayons
• Glue

Instructions:
1. Read Luke 2:52 and discuss how Jesus grew in wisdom and stature.
2. Create a timeline on a poster board showing the stages of Jesus' life.
3. Add photos or drawings of a child growing up to illustrate each stage.
4. Write key events and milestones in Jesus' life along the timeline.
5. Discuss how Jesus' growth was both physical and spiritual and how we can follow His example.

Art From The Heart

Art Projects Ages 9-12

Day 25
Luke 2:1-20 Nativity

Materials Needed:
- Clay or play dough
- Shoebox or small cardboard box
- Construction paper
- Scissors
- Glue
- Paints

Instructions:

1. Read Luke 2:1-20 and discuss the entire nativity story.

2. Use a shoebox or small cardboard box to create a stable.

3. Make clay or playdough figures of Mary, Joseph, baby Jesus, shepherds, wise men, and animals.

4. Paint and decorate the inside of the shoebox to look like a stable.

5. Arrange the figures inside the stable to complete the nativity scene.

6. Reflect on the story of Jesus' birth and the significance of each person in the nativity scene.

Art From The Heart

Once Upon Advent Tales
Family Read Aloud Fables
Little Star's Story

High above the earth, in the vast expanse of the night sky, lived a little star. This star was small and twinkled modestly among the brighter, larger stars that surrounded it. The little star often wondered if it would ever have a special purpose. He was so little and so young.

One day, a great excitement spread among the stars. The angels were preparing for a momentous event— the birth of a very special baby. The little star listened eagerly as the angels spoke of the newborn King, who would bring hope and love to the world. The star's heart filled with a longing to be part of this miraculous event. To the little star's amazement, an angel approached and spoke gently, "Little star, you have been chosen to shine brightly and lead the way to the baby Jesus. Your light will guide wise men and shepherds to the place where He lies." The little star could hardly believe it. Out of all the stars in the sky, it had been chosen for this important task.

Gathering all its courage and light, the little star began to shine as brightly as it could. Its gentle twinkle turned into a brilliant glow that pierced through the darkness of the night. Down on earth, three Wisemen saw the star and marveled at its brightness. "Look!" they exclaimed. "A new star! It must be a sign that the King of Kings has been born. Let us follow it." With gifts of gold, frankincense, and myrrh, they began their journey, guided by the little star's radiant light.

Shepherds in the fields also noticed the star's brilliance. An angel appeared to them, announcing the birth of Jesus. The shepherds, filled with awe, decided to follow the star to find the newborn King. The little star led them all to a humble stable in the town of Bethlehem. It shone directly over the stable, illuminating the place where Mary and Joseph cared for baby Jesus. As the wise men and shepherds arrived, they bowed down and offered their gifts, their hearts filled with joy and reverence.

From high above, the little star watched with a sense of fulfillment and happiness. It had played a crucial role in guiding everyone to the manger. Its light had brought people together to witness the miracle of Jesus' birth. As the night grew deeper, the little star continued to shine, its heart glowing with pride. It knew that it had been part of something truly extraordinary.

The story of its light would be told for generations, a symbol of hope and guidance for all who seek the light of love and kindness.And so, the little star remained in the sky, forever quietly now twinkling brightly, a reminder of that miraculous l night when it shone for the baby Jesus

Reflection Questions:

1. How did the little star feel when it was chosen to shine for baby Jesus?
2. What can we learn from the little star about being brave and shining our light?
3. Have you ever felt like you were too small to make a difference?
4. How can the story of the little star change your perspective?
5. In what ways can we be like the little star in our daily lives, guiding others with our kindness and love?

Art Craft Activity: Make a star Star Lantern using a jar, yellow tisue paper and a tealights.

Once Upon Advent Tales
Family Read Aloud Fables
Kevi's Good News

The Shepherds Hear the Good News (From the Perspective Of A Little Sheep)

In a peaceful field near Bethlehem, a flock of sheep grazed under the watchful eye of a young shepherd named Gershom. Among the sheep was a curious lamb named Kevi who loved to stay close to Gershom, feeling safe and protected by his presence.

One night, as Kevi was resting near Gershom, the sky suddenly lit up with a brilliant light. Kevi lifted her head and saw something extraordinary. A majestic figure appeared in the sky, shining brighter than the moon and stars. Kevi's heart raced with a mix of fear and wonder.

Gershom stood up, his eyes wide with astonishment. The figure in the sky spoke with a voice that was gentle and powerful at the same time. "Do not be afraid. I bring you good news of great joy that will be for all the people. Today in the town of David, a Savior has been born to you; He is Christ the Lord. This will be a sign to you: You will find a baby wrapped in cloths and lying in a manger."

As the angel spoke, Kevi felt a sense of calm wash over her. She nuzzled closer to Gershom, feeling his steady hand stroke her wool. The angel's message filled the air with a sense of excitement and peace.

Before Kevi could fully comprehend what was happening, the sky filled with a multitude of angels, all praising God and saying, "Glory to God in the highest, and on earth peace to men on whom His favor rests." The light and the angels slowly faded, leaving the night sky as it was before. Kevi looked up at Gershom, who was now speaking excitedly with the other shepherds. She could sense their joy and urgency as they decided to go to Bethlehem to see this miraculous event.

Gershom gently picked up Kevi and carried her, along with the other shepherds and their sheep, towards Bethlehem. The journey was filled with anticipation and hope. Kevi felt the excitement in the air as they finally arrived at a humble stable. Inside the stable, Kevi saw a baby lying in a manger, just as the angel had said. Gershom knelt beside the manger, his eyes filled with awe and wonder.

Kevi stood by his side, feeling the warmth and love that surrounded the baby Jesus.

As the shepherds shared the good news with everyone they met, Kevi knew that this night was special. She had witnessed something extraordinary, and even though she was just a little lamb, she sensed that the world would never be the same.

Reflection Question: What would you do if you were one of the shepherds who saw the angel?
Craft Activity: Create a shepherd's staff using a candy cane and ribbon.

Kevi's Good News

Once Upon Advent Tales
Family Read Aloud Fables
Through Gabriel's Eyes

High above the earth, in the heavenly realms, lived the Angel Gabriel. Gabriel was one of God's most trusted messengers, and he had carried many important messages throughout the ages. One day, God called Gabriel to His side and gave him a very special task. Gabriel's heart filled with excitement as he listened carefully to God's instructions."Gabriel," God said, "I am sending you to a young woman named Mary who lives in Nazareth. She is highly favored and will soon become the mother of My Son, Jesus. You must tell her the good news and reassure her, for she has found favor with Me."

With a sense of awe and responsibility, Gabriel bowed before God and prepared for his mission. In an instant, he left the heavenly realms and descended to earth, his wings gliding silently through the sky.

Gabriel arrived in Nazareth and found Mary in her garden, tending to her plants. He could see her gentle and kind heart shining through her every action. As Gabriel appeared before her, his radiant light filled the garden. Mary looked up, startled and frightened by the sudden appearance.

"Do not be afraid, Mary," Gabriel said softly, his voice filled with warmth and kindness. "You have found favor with God. You will conceive and give birth to a son, and you are to call him Jesus. He will be great and will be called the Son of the Most High." Mary's eyes widened with astonishment. "How can this be," she asked, "since I am not married?"

Gabriel smiled, understanding her confusion. "The Holy Spirit will come upon you, and the power of the Most High will overshadow you. So the holy one to be born will be called the Son of God. Even your relative Elizabeth is going to have a child in her old age, for no word from God will ever fail."

Mary took a deep breath, her fear turning into a profound sense of peace and acceptance. "I am the Lord's servant," she replied. "May your word to me be fulfilled." Gabriel's heart swelled with joy at Mary's faithful response. He knew that God's plan was unfolding perfectly. With a final reassuring smile, Gabriel departed, his mission accomplished.

As Gabriel ascended back to the heavenly realms, he felt a deep sense of gratitude and honor. He had delivered a message that would change the world forever. The angel's message had been received, and soon, the Son of God would be born to bring light and hope to all mankind.

Reflection Question: How do you think Mary felt when she heard the angel's message?
Craft Activity: Make an angel ornament using paper, feathers, and markers.

Through Gabriel's Eyes

<u>Once Upon Advent Tales</u>
<u>Family Read Aloud Fables</u>
<u>Benjamin's Gift</u>

Once upon a time in a faraway land, a little boy named Benjamin lived with his family. Benjamin's father was a servant to one of the Wisemen, and Benjamin admired the Wise Men for their knowledge and wisdom. One day, the Wisemen set out on a journey, following a bright star in the sky. Benjamin's father had to go with them, and he asked if Benjamin could join the caravan. To his delight, the Wisemen agreed.

As they traveled, Ben listened to the Wisemen speak of a new king, a baby born under the special star. The Wisemen were bringing precious gifts for this baby: gold, frankincense, and myrrh. Benjamin felt a pang of sadness. He wished he had something to give the baby too, but he had nothing.

Days and nights passed as they followed the star, and Ben grew more anxious. What could he offer the newborn king? He searched his small travel bag, but it was empty except for a piece of bread and a wooden carving his father had made for him. Benjamin sighed, feeling disheartened.

Finally, the star led them to a humble stable in Bethlehem. Benjamin's eyes widened in wonder as he saw the bright star shining above the place where the baby lay. The Wisemen dismounted from their camels and approached the stable, reverently carrying their gifts. Inside the stable, the air was filled with warmth and a gentle glow. Benjamin watched as the Wisemen presented their gifts to the baby Jesus, who lay in a manger. Mary and Joseph, the baby's parents, looked on with gratitude and joy.

As the Wisemen knelt before the baby, Benjamin felt a tug at his heart. He wanted to give something, anything, to show his love and respect. Suddenly, he remembered the wooden carving in his bag. It was a small, simple carving of a lamb, but it was precious to Benjamin because his father had made it for him. With a shy smile, Benjamin approached Mary. "I don't have much," he said softly, "but I want to give this to the baby."

Mary took the carving gently from Ben's hands. She looked at the little lamb and then at Benjamin, her eyes filled with warmth and kindness. "This is a beautiful gift," she said. "Thank you, Benjamin."

Benjamin's heart swelled with happiness. Mary placed the wooden lamb beside the manger, where the baby Jesus lay. Benjamin noticed that the baby's tiny hand reached out and touched the lamb and in that moment, Benjamin felt a deep sense of peace and joy.

The Wisemen smiled at Benjamin, understanding that the value of a gift is not in its material worth but in the love with which it is given. That night, in the glow of the star and the warmth of the stable, Benjamin realized that his simple gift had brought great joy to the baby and his family. As they departed, Benjamin looked back at the stable one last time. He knew he would never forget this night, the night he gave his most treasured possession to the King of Kings. And though it was a humble gift, it was given with a heart full of love.

Reflection Question: What would you give to show your love and respect for Jesus?
Craft Activity: Create a small wooden or clay carving of an animal or a special object to remind you of the importance of giving from the heart.

Once Upon Advent Tales
Family Read Aloud Fables

The Innkeeper and The Stable

In the bustling town of Bethlehem, there was an innkeeper named Reuben. He ran a small but cozy inn, and during the time of the census, his inn was filled to capacity. People from all over were arriving in Bethlehem, seeking a place to stay. Reuben and his wife, Miriam, were busy tending to the needs of their guests, making sure everyone was comfortable.

One evening, as Reuben was attending to some guests, there was a gentle knock on the door. When he opened it, he found a weary-looking man and a young woman who appeared to be tired. The man, Joseph, spoke earnestly, "Please, do you have any room for us? My wife, Mary, is about to have a baby."

Reuben's heart ached as he saw the weary couple. He glanced around the crowded inn and knew there wasn't a single bed left. "I'm so sorry," Reuben said, shaking his head. "Every room is taken. We have no place inside the inn."
Mary looked down, and Joseph sighed heavily. They turned to leave, but something in Reuben's heart stirred. He couldn't bear the thought of sending them away into the night with nowhere to go, especially with Mary so close to giving birth.

"Wait," Reuben called out, his mind racing for a solution. "I have an idea. It's not much, but you can stay in the stable out back. It's warm and dry, and at least you'll have shelter." Joseph and Mary exchanged a hopeful glance. "Thank you," Joseph said, his voice filled with gratitude. "We appreciate your kindness."

Reuben led them to the stable, a small but clean space where the animals were kept. Miriam brought fresh straw and blankets, and they did their best to make the stable as comfortable as possible. The gentle animals seemed to sense the importance of the moment and settled quietly around them.

As the night went on, the stars shone brightly above the stable. Reuben checked on Mary and Joseph periodically, making sure they were alright. He brought them food and water and offered whatever help he could. The atmosphere was filled with an unusual sense of peace and anticipation.

In the middle of the night, Miriam his wife came running to Reuben with wide eyes. "Reuben, the baby is coming! "
Reuben rushed to the stable, where he found Mary and Joseph, their faces filled with a joy. The cries of a newborn baby filled the air. Reuben felt tears welling up in his eyes as he witnessed the miracle of new life.

Mary gently wrapped the baby in cloths and laid him in a manger filled with fresh straw. She looked up at Reuben and Miriam with a grateful smile. "Thank you," she said softly. "You have given us a gift we will never forget."

Reuben felt a warmth spread through his heart. He had not offered a grand room or luxurious accommodations, but he had given what he could, and it had made all the difference. As he looked at the baby, he sensed that this was no ordinary child. There was something special, something heaven sent about him. That night, as Reuben and Miriam returned to their duties at the inn, they couldn't stop talking about the miraculous events they had witnessed. They realized that their small act of kindness had played a part in something far greater than they could have ever imagined.

In the days that followed, shepherds and wise men came to see the baby, each drawn by the same sense of wonder and awe. Reuben and Miriam welcomed them all, sharing the story of the night when the Savior of the world was born in their humble stable.

Reflection Question: What small acts of kindness can you do for others?
Craft Activity: Make a small model of a stable using craft sticks, straw, and fabric scraps to remind you of the humble place where Jesus was born.

<u>Advent & Christmas Carols For 25 LessonDays</u>

Day 1: Creation of the Promise
Song: "O Come, O Come, Emmanuel"

Day 2: Tree of Blessings
Song: "The Holly and the Ivy"

Day 3: Star of Jacob
Song: "Star of Bethlehem"

Day 4: King's Throne
Song: "Hark! The Herald Angels Sing"

Day 5: Emmanuel Ornament
Song: "Come Thou Long Expected Jesus"

Day 6: Branch of Jesse
Song: "Lo, How a Rose E'er Blooming"

Day 7: Town of Bethlehem
Song: "O Little Town of Bethlehem"

Day 8: Angel Announcement
Song: "Angels We Have Heard on High"

Day 9: Mary and Elizabeth
Song: "Mary, Did You Know?"

Day 10: Baby John
Song: "On Jordan's Bank The Baptist Cries"

Day 11: Journey Map
Song: "We Three Kings"

Day 12: Manger Scene
Song: "Away in a Manger"

Day 13: Shepherds and Sheep
Song: "While Shepherds Watched Their Flocks."

Day 14: Angel Messag
Song: "Silent Night"

Day 15: Heavenly Choir
Song: "Joy to the World"

Day 16: Shepherds' Watercolo
Song: "The First Noel"

Day 17: Wise Men's Journey
Song: "As With Gladness Men of Old"

Day 18: King Herod's Palace
Song: "Jesus What A Wonderful Child"

Day 19: Gifts of the Magi
Song: "We Three Kings"

Day 20: Escape to Egypt
Song: "God Rest Ye Merry, Gentlemen"

Day 21: Return to Nazareth
Song: " Return to Bethlehem"

Day 22: Anna's Prophecy
Song: "Light Of The World"

Day 23: Jesus in the Temple
Song: "What Child Is This?"

Day 24: Jesus' Growth
Song: "Little Drummer Boy"

Day 25: Nativity Scene
Song: "Silent Night"

Feel free to adjust or add any other songs that better fit the specific themes or your preferences for each day!

Advent Holiday Facts
"Did You Know?"

- Advent Means "Coming": The word "Advent" comes from the Latin word "adventus," which means "coming" or "arrival." It's all about getting ready for Jesus' arrival!

- Advent Begins on Sunday: Advent always starts on a Sunday, four weeks before Christmas Day, and lasts until Christmas Eve.

- The Advent Wreath: The Advent wreath has four candles, one for each week of Advent. The candles are often colored purple, pink, and white. Each week's candle represents hope, peace, joy, and love.

- The Purple and Pink Colors: The purple candles represent repentance and preparation. The pink candle, lit on the third Sunday, is called the "Gaudete" candle, which means "Rejoice!"

- A Fifth Candle: Some Advent wreaths also have a white candle in the center called the "Christ Candle," which is lit on Christmas Eve or Christmas Day.

- Advent Calendars: The tradition of Advent calendars began in Germany in the 19th century. Each day, a door opens to reveal a picture or a small treat.

- The Jesse Tree: The Jesse Tree is a special Advent tradition where each day you add a new ornament that represents a Bible story leading up to Jesus' birth.

- St. Nicholas Day: December 6th is St. Nicholas Day, celebrating Santa Claus. Some families use this day to give small gifts or treats.

-

- Advent Hymns: Many traditional Advent hymns, like "O Come, O Come, Emmanuel," are based on ancient Christian songs that were used for hundreds of years.

- Advent in Different Countries: In some countries, Advent is celebrated with special foods. For example, in Sweden, people eat "pepparkakor" (gingerbread cookies) during Advent.

- The Advent Star: In some cultures, families decorate their homes with a star to symbolize the Star of Bethlehem that guided the Wisemen to Jesus.

- Advent's Meaning in Different Christian Traditions: While many Christians celebrate Advent, some traditions emphasize different aspects of the season, like preparing spiritually or focusing on different Bible stories.

- The O Antiphons: During the last seven days of Advent, the "O Antiphons" are sung or said in prayers. Each one starts with "O" and describes a name or title for Jesus.

Advent Holiday Facts
"Did You Know?"

- **Advent in the Old Testament:** The idea of waiting and preparing for a special event is not new. The Old Testament has stories of waiting for the Messiah, which Advent helps to remember.

- **A Time for Charity:** Advent is a time when many people focus on giving to others. Some families create "Advent Giving" calendars with different charitable acts for each day.

- **No Purple in Advent's Origin:** Originally, Advent was a time of fasting and preparation, and purple was a symbol of penance. Over time, it evolved into a joyful preparation for Christmas.

- **Early Christian Advent:** Early Christians celebrated Advent as a time to prepare for both Christmas and the second coming of Christ, making it a time of reflection and anticipation.

- **Advent Songs for Kids:** Many children's Christmas songs, like "Jingle Bells" and "Frosty the Snowman," are not actually Advent songs, but they are enjoyed during the Christmas season!

- **Nativity Scenes:** Some families set up nativity scenes early during Advent, but traditionally, the figures of the Wisemen are added only on January 6th, the Feast of the Epiphany.

- **Advent and Christmas Traditions:** In some cultures, the Advent season ends with a big celebration called "Epiphany" on January 6th, which celebrates the visit of the Wise Men.

- **The Advent Wreath's Symbolism:** Each part of the Advent wreath has a special meaning. The circular shape represents God's eternal love, and the greenery symbolizes eternal life.

- **Advent in Australia:** Since December is summer in Australia, many Australian families celebrate Advent with outdoor activities and Christmas picnics.

- **Advent Letters:** In some traditions, children write letters to Santa Claus/St. Nicholas during Advent, sharing their wishes and hopes for the holiday season.

- **Advent and Family Time:** Advent is a special time for families to come together, read Bible stories, sing songs, and prepare their hearts for Christmas.

- **The Advent Fast:** In some Christian traditions, Advent was originally a period of fasting similar to Lent, where people would prepare spiritually for Christmas through prayer and reflection.

Advent Facts Old & New

Advent And Christmas Storyteller Books

A Tabby Cats Blessing: Yoshi's Christmas Tale Of Love
https://www.amazon.com/dp/B0D7W5JHFJ

Christmas Quiz Game Book
https://www.amazon.com/Christmas-Quiz-Game-Book-Occasion-ebook/dp/B00AICU4QO/

Twelve Days Of Christmas Quiz Book
https://www.amazon.com/Twelve-Days-Christmas-Quiz-Game-ebook/dp/B00ARN4THU/

Christmas Quiz Book: Complete Holiday Edition
https://www.amazon.com/Christmas-Quiz-Game-Book-Complete-ebook/dp/B00GSC8U7Y/

The Storyteller Shop

The Storyteller Shop